High-Five Teaching
K–5

Rich Allen dedicates this book to his three favorite young learners:
Pippa, Kathryn, and Angela.

Cindy Rickert dedicates this book to three important people:
My mother, Gina, who supported my journey as a Green Light teacher;
my young daughter, Leilani, who one day will hopefully experience
a Green Light classroom; and finally to a true Green Light teacher,
Emma Jeter, for jumping head first into the creative pool with me.

High-Five Teaching
K–5

**Using Green Light
Strategies to
Create Dynamic,
Student-Focused
Classrooms**

Rich Allen
Cindy Rickert

CORWIN
A SAGE Company

For information:

Corwin
A SAGE Company
2455 Teller Road
Thousand Oaks, California 91320
(800) 233-9936
Fax: (800) 417-2466
www.corwin.com

SAGE Ltd.
1 Oliver's Yard
55 City Road
London EC1Y 1SP
United Kingdom

SAGE Pvt. Ltd.
B 1/I 1 Mohan Cooperative
   Industrial Area
Mathura Road, New Delhi 110 044
India

SAGE Asia-Pacific Pte. Ltd.
33 Pekin Street #02-01
Far East Square
Singapore 048763

Printed in the United States of America

Library of Congress Cataloging-in-Publication Data

Allen, Rich, 1957 Sept. 28-
High-five teaching, K-5: using green light strategies to create dynamic, student-focused classrooms / Rich Allen and Cindy Rickert.
    p. cm.
Includes bibliographical references and index.
ISBN 978-1-4129-8112-5 (pbk.)

   1. Elementary school teaching—United States. 2. Student-centered learning—United States. 3. Motivation in education—United States. I. Rickert, Cindy. II. Title.

LB1555.A56 2010
372.1102   2010016129

This book is printed on acid-free paper.

10   11   12   13   14   10   9   8   7   6   5   4   3   2   1

Acquisitions Editor:	Jessica Allan
Associate Editor:	Joanna Coelho
Editorial Assistant:	Allison Scott
Production Editor:	Veronica Stapleton
Copy Editor:	Adam Dunham
Typesetter:	C&M Digitals (P) Ltd.
Proofreader:	Dennis W. Webb
Indexer:	Molly Hall
Cover Designer:	Rose Storey

Cartoons on pages 1, 4, 6, 13, 15, 22, 27, 30, 39, 40, 44, 46, 53, 63, 66, 68, 77, 89, 119, 123, 159, 181
© Green Light Education, LLC. Used by permission.

Contents

Preface

The Story of Cindy

As an educational consultant for 25 years, I've worked with tens of thousands of teachers from all over the world—in almost every U.S. state and throughout Europe, Asia, Australasia, Russia, and the Middle East. As you can imagine, the educators I meet teach different subjects to students of all ages, hailing from a wide variety of cultures and very different socioeconomic backgrounds. Despite this diversity, from downtown New York to the outback of Australia, the schools and districts I work with have remarkably similar needs: Their teachers are reaching out for new ideas and strategies to make their classrooms more effective—to better engage students, to improve learning outcomes, and to make teaching less combative and more collaborative. It seems that, no matter where they live on this increasingly connected planet, kids are united in their disconnection from traditional teaching practices (Klein, 2008).

This is why I developed the *Green Light* approach to teaching—simply meaning something different from "chalk and talk." Green Light strategies are dynamic, interactive, and fun, but they have a very serious premise: They are designed to maximize student recall and understanding by drawing on the latest brain-based educational research.

In 2006, my travels brought me to Virginia Beach, Virginia. In attendance were two young fifth-grade inclusion-level teaching partners, Cindy Rickert and Emma Jeter. As they confessed to me later, Cindy and Emma had signed up for the course merely as a means of picking up their required professional development points for the year. They actually had no interest in the course material.

All that changed after the first day of the workshop, which demonstrated a variety of practical ideas for dynamic teaching. Inspired and excited by strategies they believed would engage their reluctant students, Cindy and Emma talked late into the night about a plan to radically change their classrooms. Ignoring my suggestion to gradually incorporate the strategies, they decided to start the new school year with a bang: They would build a new classroom format from the ground up, changing their physical environments, teaching styles, and lesson plans. Unbeknown to me, they left my workshop to begin a complete classroom makeover—starting with moving furniture and painting on the floor!

By the time the 2006–2007 school year started, their classrooms physically looked different from the previous year, sounded different from other classrooms in their building, and—most important—felt different to the students. Encouraged by their principal, Cindy and Emma created a safe learning environment where learning was fun, where every lesson had a sound track, and where every student had a chance to succeed. To their intense satisfaction, the level of student engagement, and academic results, in their classrooms started to improve rapidly.

Inspired by this early success, Cindy and Emma became "conspirators in creativity," challenging each other and working together to design and develop new approaches to teach information in ways that were both enjoyable to students at the time and highly effective in the long run. Kids who had largely been given up on by the school started to achieve. Attendance, literacy, and numeracy soared.

That year was a success in many ways and on many levels—for the two teachers as well as their students. However—right or wrong—these days in education, success is measured by test results. And here is where the best evidence of their efforts emerged. Cindy's and Emma's students passed the year-ending Virginia Standards of Learning exams at extraordinary levels. Students who had *never passed a single standardized test in their lives* not only passed but achieved high marks in many categories as well. The experiment of pulling the new strategies together into a focused approach to dynamic teaching was a stunning educational triumph.

In the middle of that school year, I began research for a new book, consulting hundreds of teachers who were already using dynamic teaching strategies about their most successful new lesson ideas. Cindy and Emma contributed several keys lessons to this book, *Green Light Classrooms: Teaching Techniques That Accelerate Learning* (Allen, 2008).

After that first year, Cindy chose to remain in teaching while Emma left to devote herself to being a full-time mother. Cindy continued to develop her new teaching ideas, enabling her bottom-stream students to achieve outstanding test results year after year. I stayed in touch, watching her progress with interest, and eventually we began to copresent at workshops and conferences.

At these events, during our constant conversations about education, I began to realize that Cindy has terrific, natural instincts about how to keep students engaged. I often asked her why she had introduced a particular new strategy in her classroom, and she would frequently reply, "I'm not really sure—I just tried it, it worked, so I keep doing it!" My workshop had given Cindy a handful of ideas, but she had run with them—coming up with hundreds of practical new applications and approaches. At that point, her new ideas weren't based on educational research or theory; Cindy was merely relying on her instincts to create the best possible learning conditions for her students. And, they were working with astonishing results.

I was amazed at the accuracy of her instincts in establishing and maintaining an effective learning environment and their alignment with current research about student-engagement strategies and brain research. Essentially, this is why I have asked Cindy to share her ideas with you in this book.

As coauthors, our aim is to help you to replicate Cindy's success—to establish a dynamic classroom, quickly, and for very little, if any, cost. Thus, this book takes the ideas, strategies, and techniques Cindy developed to transform her fifth-grade classroom and expands them into a widely adaptable strategies for any elementary teacher, at all grade levels. It's a practical how-to guide for anyone who wants to dramatically improve educational outcomes and has the courage to try something different.

We believe every elementary teacher can transform his or her own classroom into a dynamic learning experience for their students, leading to the same results Cindy is now experiencing in her classroom year after year.

This belief is based on an important premise: If the conditions for success are properly set in place and orchestrated throughout the year, *every child can learn.*

As Cindy's three-year experiment proves, if you create a dynamic learning environment, *all* of your students—no matter what their educational challenges—will achieve a measure of success beyond both your and their expectations (Jensen, 2006; Jiaxu & Weiyi, 2000; Rossi, 2002). And, you will create a positive learning spiral that builds confidence in the most reluctant learners—giving them the ultimate educational gift: hope.

Acknowledgments

The authors wish to thank the following people for their valuable contributions to the development of this project:

- Our editor, Karen Pryor, for giving endlessly of her time, energy, and editing wisdom in all aspects of the design, evolution, and eventual maturation of this manuscript. You are indeed a stunningly gifted and talented writing "moose." We are both deeply indebted to you for many aspects of this book. Simply put, without you, it would not exist.
- Our illustrator, Wayne Logue, for providing insightful, illuminating, and inspirational illustrations that both underscore and clarify so many of the key ideas presented here.
- Our early-feedback team, Ann Kerby, Jenn Currie, Cheryl Dick, Tom Gannon, Tiffany Reindl, and Sue Tomaszewski, for offering us some initial advice and input regarding the structure, flow, and articulation of the concepts and ideas we are trying to communicate.
- Our researcher, Cheryl Dick, for taking the time to carefully gather the most up-to-date citations that best support our theories, hypotheses, and claims about effective teaching strategies.

PUBLISHER'S ACKNOWLEDGMENTS

Corwin gratefully acknowledges the contributions of the following reviewers:

Jacie Maslyk
Elementary Principal
Crafton Elementary School
Pittsburgh, PA

About the Authors

Photo by Ted Davis

Rich Allen, PhD, is a highly regarded educator with more than 25 years experience coaching teachers. Founder and president of Green Light Education, he is the author of numerous popular educational books, including most recently *High-Impact Teaching Strategies for the 'XYZ' Era of Education* (2010), *Green Light Classrooms: Teaching Techniques That Accelerate Learning* (2008), and *TrainSmart: Effective Trainings Every Time* (2008, 2nd ed.).

He has taken his dynamic instructional strategies beyond the United States and Canada to such diverse countries as the United Kingdom, Australia, New Zealand, Hong Kong, Singapore, Thailand, Brunei, Russia, Jordan, and Brazil. Dr. Allen is also a popular keynote speaker at international education conferences and works with schools and school districts to embed effective teaching methods into mainstream curriculum.

Dr. Allen first took to the stage as an off-Broadway actor, before starting his educational career as a high school math and drama teacher. In 1985, he became a lead facilitator for SuperCamp (an accelerated-learning program for teens) and has since worked with more than 25,000 students worldwide. Dr. Allen completed his doctorate in educational psychology at Arizona State University, where he studied how the human brain receives, processes, and recalls information—knowledge that informs all aspects of his teaching strategies. The author resides in the U.S. Virgin Islands on the sun-kissed paradise of St Croix; he can be reached at his e-mail address: rich@drrichallen.com.

Photo by
David Adam Beloff

Cindy Rickert teaches fifth grade in an inclusive setting in Virginia Beach, Virginia. In her 10 years of teaching fifth graders of varying levels, she has taught students with ADHD (attention deficit hyperactivity disorder) and ODD (oppositional defiant disorder) as well as those who have autism and are identified as EMR (educable mentally retarded), ESOL (English speakers of other languages), and intellectually gifted. She is specially trained and has state certification as an ESOL teacher and is actively pursuing a doctorate-level degree in education. Recognized as her school's 2008 Reading Teacher of the Year and a model teacher in Virginia Beach since 2002, Cindy is active in mentoring and teacher training for the Virginia Beach public school system. She has represented her city in state-test standard-setting committees and has created training videos for her district. Her lessons and strategies have been published in nationally circulated books, and she travels around the country teaching those strategies. She has seen both her students with special needs' and her general-education students' test scores soar since her decision to incorporate movement, memory strategies, and music in her classroom.

Introduction

TEACHERS MAKE ALL OTHER PROFESSIONS POSSIBLE.

This book provides tools to help teachers create a Green Light classroom. So, let's start by defining what it means to use a "Green Light"—versus a "red light"—approach to teaching.

The term *Green Light* comes from the book *Green Light Classrooms: Teaching Techniques That Accelerate Learning* (Allen, 2008), which contrasts two types of teaching styles:

- **Red Light**—meaning a traditional, lecture-saturated educational approach that ultimately stops students from learning; this is an approach that dampens students' enthusiasm for education because it does not meet their needs.
- **Green Light**—meaning the opposite: a focus on finding new and creative ways to teach, primarily addressing the fact that the digital natives in our classrooms learn differently, which means that *our teaching strategies must also be different.*

The Green Light approach is not a rigid teaching philosophy. It doesn't insist on a series of specific teaching practices that are the *only way.* Instead, it's a flexible approach that encourages educators to look for different ways of teaching, to focus on "what works" with their students, and to build on success. In doing so, it challenges many traditional teaching ideas, such as:

This is how I was taught. It worked for me, so it will work with my students.

I said it, so now they know it.

Teachers should talk more than students.

If kids are bored, it's their problem.

You don't have to teach students how to remember.

The key to teaching is crowd control.

Instead, the Green Light approach is based on the idea that learning can and should be fun. Green Light teachers understand that many elementary students can't make sense of or remember information unless they engage with it physically, socially, and emotionally. They know that the worst thing about a bored student is not that they are more likely to act out but that they have *stopped learning.* And Green Light teachers deliberately teach memory skills. They don't just give tests; they show their students how to succeed brilliantly when taking a test.

The starting point for adopting this teaching approach is outlined in the *Green Light Classrooms* book, which provides nine *themes* for teachers to weave into their lessons:

1. **Memory:** Pegs, association, body location, acrostics, and rhyming

2. **Connections:** Creating meaning; allowing students to own the material

3. **Movement:** Physically engaging students in the learning process

4. **Novelty:** Harnessing something *different* to capture students' attention

5. **Tone:** Music, chants, and teacher's tonal changes and pauses

6. **Emotion:** Using laughter and surprise to fire curiosity and excitement

7. **Socialization:** Student-to-student discussions, processing, and debriefs

8. **Drama:** Theatrics, story telling, and students acting out the learning

9. **Visuals:** Posters, mind maps, doodles, and drawing

Green Light Classrooms also includes a series of proven, real-life lessons showing how educators around the world are incorporating these themes into their teaching practice. Each lesson shows how the teacher used to present a lesson, outlines their new Green Light approach, and records the often-dramatic results this produced. The lessons are highly creative—and startlingly, often radically, different.

And herein lies an issue: Feedback from the book shows that, while teachers find the lesson ideas inspiring, some are hesitant to make such radical changes. These teachers can see the potential of the strategies and understand in theory why Green Light works, but the leap into the unknown seems too risky.

They might read the preface to this book and point out that Cindy and Emma were emboldened by the confidence of youth, motivated by each other, and lucky enough to have a visionary principal in the right place at the right time. They might also quite correctly suggest that not all teachers would—or could—devote a significant amount of their summer vacation to developing the physical environment, techniques, procedures, and rituals required to bring the Green Light approach to life in their classrooms.

This book short-circuits that process by sharing years of thinking, ideas, and practical strategies for setting up a Green Light classroom. If you are interested in incorporating the Green Light themes into your classroom, this book will show you step-by-step strategies for weaving them into any content area, for elementary students of any age.

In doing so, it builds a bridge between theory and practice, starting with the *High-Five Principles* that underpin every second of Cindy's teaching time. The book then offers you detailed instructions for laying the foundations for Green Light teaching with your students in the first week of the school year, in Chapter 6, titled "Five-by-Five." This is the educational equivalent of "tilling the soil" before you spread the seeds of learning. By taking the time and trouble to prepare your students for a different way of learning, you will achieve faster and better results. The book then gives you a series of Cindy's actual lesson plans to show you how the principles work in practice. Finally, it provides a *High-Five Toolkit* with detailed materials and instructions to support you in introducing the core new-teaching strategies.

HIGH FIVE
PRINCIPLES

Theory
Green Light
themes,
techniques,
and
strategies

Practice

BRIDGING
THE GAP BETWEEN
THEORY AND PRACTICE

Before we get into the High-Five Principles, let's take a step back and consider *why* we should go to all this trouble. Changing the way you teach is a big thing to ask. It takes time and effort. So, why can't we keep teaching in the same way? What's wrong with traditional, red light teaching?

What's wrong is the simple fact that many kids *do not learn* information presented in the traditional red light, "chalk and talk" teaching style. Despite widespread acceptance that students have different learning styles—and volumes of brain-based education research highlighting the consequent need for new education styles using movement, socialization, music, and memory strategies—the most common method of information delivery in most primary classrooms remains lecture, supported by information written on the board and worksheets. Yet, for many children—even bright ones—this form of education *does not work.* And, when kids who *can* learn are prevented from doing so, it causes terrible damage.

Here's a real-life example: A truly bright elementary student started school filled with excitement and, initially, proved to be an excellent student. Her kindergarten and first-grade reports extolled her intelligence and academic progress. All was well until, in second grade, she started failing her spelling tests. Her teacher told her to learn the spelling words by writing them out; so, every evening the little girl conscientiously practiced her spelling list. But it didn't matter how many times she wrote out the words; they just didn't stick in her head. One day, clutching yet another bad test result, the little girl announced she "wasn't good at learning." Appalled, her mother helped her with a different way of learning the spelling words: some simple memory techniques—rhymes and associations (Jensen, 2008a)—which seemed to help the spelling words stick in her head. But when the little girl came home the next day with her 20/20 results, she still looked troubled.

"Honey, what's wrong? You did great!" said her mother.

"Yes, but I cheated," was the girl's downhearted reply.

Her mother was astonished: "Why do you think that?"

"Because that new way we learned the words . . . it was easy and fun."

Within a single year, this enthusiastic student had been taught a powerful (yet highly destructive) lesson: Learning is difficult and boring. Once students lose faith in their ability to learn—and our ability to make education enjoyable—we might as well shut our schools and go home.

"DAM" THOSE KIDS!

Young children arrive at school bursting with energy and enthusiasm. Yet, most elementary teaching strategies focus directly and unashamedly on squashing their natural exuberance. Lively boys, in constant motion on the playground, are made to sit still; noisy girls, who never stop talking outside school, are told to be quiet; artistic kids are reprimanded for doodling in their margins; creative minds are told there is only *one* way.

In effect, traditional teaching practices build an educational "dam": they keep in check the natural energy students bring to the classroom, in the process killing off their ability and enthusiasm for learning. Ironically, this massive effort to pen in and control their students requires teachers to

expend enormous amounts of energy themselves—energy that might be much better spent designing new and creative lessons or helping students actually learn.

Green Light teaching breaches the dam. It allows the natural energy of students to power the learning process, creating a cascade effect, an education stream that turns into a river of knowledge. As teachers, we shouldn't try to dam this stream: Why struggle against the forces of nature? Our job is to let the stream flow and help it to find its easiest path.

This is not to suggest that Green Light teaching advocates a lack of control. In fact, many of its strategies are all about guiding and controlling the flow of learning—removing obstacles and making sure it's going in the right direction. Red light teachers may feel they're in control as they dam their students' energy; but, in fact, they are creating the potential for the dam to burst at its weakest point. This results in a chaotic explosion that can quickly descend into anarchy. In contrast, Green Light teaching releases kids' energy in a controlled way, by deliberately creating channels for learning. Like the babbling brook, Green Light classrooms may be noisy at times and certainly involve lots of movement—but they are not chaotic. Everything has a purpose, and that purpose is effective learning.

To continue this metaphor a little further, the "dam the kids" approach to teaching requires constant nervous bursts of energy from the teacher to keep the dam walls from crumbling—while the class stagnates behind the illusion of control. (They may be sitting still and quiet; but are they learning?) For teachers, this constant battle to retain the wall of control is tiring; for students, it is tedious; for both, it is an inefficient and unproductive way of learning.

By contrast, once you remove the dam—by building movement, socialization, fun, and music into your classroom—you release kids' natural energy to fuel the learning process (Jensen, 2006). With everyone working in the same direction, the classroom becomes less of a battleground. Teachers don't have to fight for control, students regain their enthusiasm for learning, and the results speak for themselves.

This sounds great in theory, but how does it work in practice? How do we make sure that, as we open the floodgates of the dam, the unleashed energy flows in the right direction? The following High-Five Principles—the central tenets of this book—will help you to enlist your students as collaborators in the learning process and focus their pent-up energy on achieving educational outcomes.

And so, with apologies to Obi-Wan Kenobi, here are the Principles that will help you *"Use the force for good . . ."*

Principle 1: True Learning Communities: Students Taking Responsibility

Students have a wealth of time, energy, enthusiasm, and focus they can potentially bring to any classroom situation. But, how do we get them to invest these precious resources into the learning process? The starting point is to bring students onto our side of the table: by *offering choice* and *sharing responsibility.* By giving students real input into the learning process, we create a solid, supportive classroom community (Marzano, 2007).

Principle 2: Optimum Learning Conditions: Creating Safety and Security

To get everyone working in the same direction, students must trust their teacher—*and each other* (Tomlinson, 2008). We must therefore deliberately build trust from the very first moment of the very first day of school and carefully monitor and maintain it throughout the year. In a high-threat learning situation, where students feel at risk of looking stupid, few are willing to participate. When a student makes a mistake, we can choose to turn it into a destructive moment of humiliation or a powerful learning experience. Making students feel secure is about choosing the second option. If your students trust you, they will be willing to take risks, and they will not be afraid to make the mistakes that will teach them the most valuable lessons (Gray, Braver, & Raichle 2002; Wessler, 2004.)

Principle 3: Teaching to the Moment: Working Within *Their* World

Like water, students find their own level. Our carefully thought through lesson plan may be perfect in theory, but the moment we start teaching it, every assumption is tested to the limit. Numerous factors can affect the way a lesson actually pans out, including student interest, environment, mood, and energy levels. This is why we should consider our lesson plans as fluid suggestions rather than concrete constructs. We don't have to chain ourselves to a predetermined structure—if it's not working. Conscientious teachers are *conscious* teachers—letting student interest guide the lesson, constantly checking in, and confidently changing gears to take the lesson to a different—but more appropriate—level than planned. Sometimes, this might mean we don't cover all the material—and sometimes we will cover more. Either way, it doesn't matter. The highest priority is to seize the moments when our students are highly engaged and interested and teach into these precious educational opportunities (Hersh, 2009).

Principle 4. Learning Beyond Listening: Linking Action and Understanding

Learning by doing is the most effective way for students to develop an understanding of any new concept. "Lecture and listen" teaching—while still effective if used *infrequently* and *briefly*—is essentially an outdated educational strategy. Very few elementary students learn best by sitting in a chair and listening to a grown-up. Their natural learning style is more likely to be through physical participation, application, peer observation, or conversation. As teachers, we can harness student energy by finding ways to connect action—physical and social engagement—to the learning process (Allington, 2006.)

Principle 5. The Learning Spiral: Building Success on Success

The most powerful force for binding your students to the learning process is success. In the classroom, *current* success always drives *future* success: The positive platform of accomplishment becomes the springboard for diving confidently into subsequent lessons. Thus, our final principle for guiding students involves actively working to ensure every student *does* succeed—by using smaller learning steps, novel teaching practices, and deliberate memory strategies—and by publicly celebrating and acknowledging any and every level of learning success. When celebrating success becomes a classroom custom, we create a positive learning spiral that keeps students highly motivated (Marzano, 2007).

What About Technology?

If you are lucky enough to have technology of any kind in your classroom (computers, interactive whiteboards, iPods, digital cameras, etc.), be sure to use it wherever possible to support the above Principles. Because not every school can afford technology, the key examples in this book avoid relying on expensive equipment. However, you'll find a table at the end of each Principle dedicated to specific ideas for using technology. Think of this as a springboard to get you started.

Bear in mind that using technology in the classroom does more than improve digital literacy (Cookson, 2009). Far more exciting, for Green Light teachers, is the potential for technology to engage nontraditional learners. Research shows the effective use of technology as a teaching tool actually enhances the learning process itself, creating a new level of engagement, extending thinking, and encouraging creativity—particularly in reluctant students (O'Rourke & Fletcher, 2004). This is why Green Light teachers use technology whenever possible. It's an opportunity to meet digital natives on their own turf—a quick and easy means of creating a safe and highly engaging learning environment.

FOOD FOR THOUGHT

Before you start to explore the following chapters, here are three important ideas to bear in mind.

First, each year, Cindy has a number of students with special needs in her classroom. While the strategies listed in this book work extremely well with this population, this *does not* mean they are designed for bottom-stream students. Using the principles will help your students to achieve better learning outcomes—regardless of their IQ or natural ability. In a Green Light classroom, your more-able students will shine even more brightly, while students who find learning challenging will achieve success—often for the first time.

Second, don't be fooled into thinking about strategies in this book as "energizers." Just because many of the strategies are about making learning enjoyable, this does not mean you should only bring them out when kids are bored. In a Green Light classroom, these strategies are the basis for teaching *everything!* They should underpin every moment of the school day.

Third, this book contains hundreds of tried and trusted techniques and ideas that work in Cindy's classroom. But, they may not all work for *your* students in *everything* you teach *all* of the time. When implementing the strategies, take an experimental approach. Try a technique, and if it works, keep it—and then build on it. If not, try something else. In practice, most teachers find the "70/30 rule" applies. In other words, you'll likely be able to fill about 70% of your lessons with the specific techniques you find in this book—as they are. The other 30% will come from your own ideas, adaptations, and adjustments.

The key is not to get hung up thinking of these strategies being the *only way*. The principles explained in this book will hold true—no matter what your teaching situation. But, the strategies suggested to implement them, while proven in one classroom, may need some tiny adjustments to work well in yours. Ultimately, your teaching situation is uniquely dependent on addressing the needs of your students. So, take the ideas in this book, but mix them with your own knowledge, understanding, and background. The result will be a tailored teaching approach that delivers the best learning outcomes in *your* classroom for *your* students.

Are *You* Having Fun Yet?

As you implement the strategies you decide on, there's a very simple acid test for making sure they're working: Are *you* having fun with them? One of the incredibly positive side effects of Green Light teaching is that educators begin to enjoy themselves. They actually start looking forward to going to school.

In fact, Green Light teaching is as beneficial for educators as it is for students. Engaged kids are so much easier and more rewarding to teach because they stop acting out and start participating. If you're harnessing students' energy, you don't have to expend so much of your own. If you don't have to deal with discipline issues, your day is infinitely more pleasant. And finally, if your students achieve, so do you.

If you finish each day knowing you've helped children become successful learners—rather than simply surviving another round of "dam" crowd control—then life is more meaningful, richer, and more satisfying. Green Light teaching, as implemented through the High-Five Principles shown here, will help you remember *why* you became an educator in the first place: to make a difference in the world by giving every child the chance to succeed.

1

True Learning Communities

Students Taking Responsibility

Breach the Dam! A natural step in the course of any child's development is taking charge of her life and becoming her own person. Instead of attempting to dominate and control them in the classroom, we can consciously channel students' desire for control into taking charge of the classroom environment, thus both encouraging this process while simultaneously creating a more productive and positive classroom experience.

OVERVIEW

Students have a wealth of time, energy, enthusiasm, and focus they could potentially bring to any classroom situation. But, how do we get them to invest these precious resources into the learning process? The starting point is to bring students onto our side of the table, by *offering choice* and *sharing responsibility*. By giving students real input into the learning process, we create a solid, supportive classroom community.

Offering choice to young learners is not a common theme in education. In many schools, "good" behavior is equated with students mindlessly obeying commands. While this may be better than anarchy, it has nothing to do with learning. Teaching is not crowd control: It's about firing up young minds—not beating them into submission.

Red light classrooms are essentially run like kingdoms. The King (or Queen, as is frequently the case in many elementary classrooms) has full control and makes all the important decisions. From a Green Light perspective, there are many problems with this arrangement in terms of teachers, students, and learning outcomes.

Total Control Exhausts Teachers

The feudal classroom is tough on teachers. For one thing, it takes a huge amount of effort to maintain control and order. In our kingdom example, monarchs rule by force, spending huge amounts of resources on maintaining their armies. Security and defending the realm are the monarch's highest priority. Arming the troops is more important than feeding the people. In a classroom, red light teachers are essentially making the same resourcing decisions. If a large portion of the teacher's time and energy is spent purely on maintaining proper order, then, clearly, the teacher will have less time and energy to spend on any actual teaching.

Here's a challenging thought: If all teachers created a learning community in their classrooms, *we could discard a significant portion of teachers' professional development*. Every year, we expend an incredible amount of energy on teaching both new and experienced teachers "better classroom-management techniques." But, the primary focus of most of these techniques is controlling students or "damming their energy."

If our classroom systems supported choice and gave students responsibility for learning, would we need classroom-management strategies? Could we take the time, energy, and money spent on teaching educators negative control techniques and invest it in developing better learning strategies?

This wouldn't just be better for students, it would also remove massive stress from teachers. If the teacher is the only person responsible for managing the classroom, this puts her under a vast and unnecessary pressure. Most of us can manage to be fair and reasonable most of the time. But, everyone has bad days. When we are under stress, our ability to keep order breaks down. Typically, we either allow our mood to permeate the classroom (dragging our students down with us) or we simply don't have the energy to maintain order—and our students sense this and run riot. What we need to realize is that we don't *have* to take on the whole responsibility. We can share it with our students, thereby setting aside a hugely stressful burden.

It's possible to create a classroom community that makes better use of everyone's time and energy, puts teachers in touch with their students,

and reduces the stress created by discipline issues. All we have to do is give up our crowns and tap into our students' seemingly endless energy by inviting them to join us in running the classroom. By proactively and consciously allowing students to become a significant part of what happens in their classroom community, we can focus more of our own energy on creating and delivering dynamic lessons.

Offering Choice Improves Learning Outcomes

When teachers share control with students, test results improve because having ownership of the education process allows learners to make the choices that will be most beneficial to their success. Also, students are more likely to be engaged with and proactive and enthusiastic about classroom activities they chose, as opposed to those foisted upon them by their teacher. And together, these factors increase attention, understanding, and retention (Glasser, 1999).

At a more philosophical level, giving students choice also lays the foundation for critical thinking. Today's students get little value from learning facts they can find on Google in less than three seconds. But, they derive a huge advantage from high-level decision-making and critical-thinking skills. Anyone can look up facts and dates. We don't need someone who knows the date the bomb was dropped on Hiroshima; we need a thinker who can decide what they will do to promote world peace. As a society, we should be developing people who are comfortable with taking control of their destinies (Winger, 2009).

The growth of this characteristic starts in the earliest years of a child's development. It is not a talent we suddenly acquire at the age of 18 or 21. The art of learning from mistakes and making good decisions is a *life-long process*—and one that many adults fail to master. It requires us to make our own decisions and discover which ones were correct (Whew!), which ones were incorrect (Yikes!), and what we would do different next time. This is a long and often-treacherous process that requires constant practice and guidance. Only when students are allowed to make as many of their own decisions as early as possible will they evolve this skill to the point where they make useful decisions most of the time.

This course of development is already well under way by the time children reach kindergarten. They have been learning to make decisions every day, sometimes on their own, often with a parent's or sibling's guidance. So, when students arrive in our classrooms, we have to make a choice: Will we attempt to squash this natural process of development in them, or will we encourage it?

The Green Light choice is to look for ways to actively promote this vital developmental path because when students make more of their own choices and take more responsibility, *they change emotionally.* This emotional shift takes them from *reacting* to a situation in which they feel trapped to *proactively* taking their places in the world.

The difference between these two emotional vantage points simply cannot be overstated—it's huge. The first drives students to act out and to disrespect their peers and teachers as they struggle to maintain a sense of identity in their world. The second is empowering, allowing students the freedom to learn new and powerful decision-making strategies as they revel in being a significant, vital, and essential part of their world. By consciously supporting this process, Green Light teachers underpin the overarching goal of all education—producing better-developed, emotionally mature students who become happier, more-productive adults.

Replace Teacher Directions With Student Decisions

Offering choices makes the student responsible for the lesson. No longer is it a *teacher direction,* but a *student decision.* This does not mean students are ready to take charge of their lives and make every decision for themselves. Nor does it mean your students will always make the best decisions. If they make decisions that won't work for the class, you can always exert control to get back on track. For example, in picking groups, if the groups are not to your satisfaction, find a reason to ask students to pick again until you have the groups you want. Or simply allow some opportunities for students to pick their own groups, and other times make these choices for them.

But, there are a surprising number of decisions students are capable of making by themselves, and many more they can sensibly make with appropriate guidance from a teacher. Wherever we can, we need to let them make those decisions. If we include, guide, and empower our students by allowing them to make simple everyday choices, we create vested team members, not robots.

While this may look like giving up control, it is simply leading from behind. As Nelson Mandela said, "A leader is like a shepherd. He stays behind the flock, letting the most nimble go out ahead, whereupon the others follow, not realizing that all along they are being directed from behind" (Mandela, 1995).

Think about it for a moment: What does it matter *how* students learn, as long as they do? If letting go of surface "control" helps your students to learn, doesn't it actually put you in true control in terms of meeting the lesson's objective?

Reexamine Classroom Rules

Take a look at the practical difference between students taking responsibility and the common teaching approach where teachers cling onto control. Let's take classroom rules as an example. In traditional red light classrooms, rules are often already posted on the walls (ominously, in bold print) as students arrive for the all-important first day of school. One of the first things the teacher does is carefully review them with the students and describe in excruciating detail the penalties that will follow if any rule is broken. And, thus, the classroom tone is set.

Rules that are presented as mandates from above will always be a problem. If we impose them on students, they have no meaning. They become just one more thing students are being told: Except for fearing reprimand, the students are not connected to the rules in any real or relevant way.

By contrast, in a Green Light classroom, the idea of classroom rules is handled in a different way. As you will see later in more detail in the Five-by-Five chapter of this book, you can *create rules with your students* at the end of your first week. You need to wait this long because it takes time to build a classroom dynamic that encourages trust and sharing. By then, you'll have modeled appropriate classroom behavior, so you'll get the sort of rules you were hoping for!

Or, to take this thought one step further, many Green Light teachers believe that if the rules can implicitly be learned by the students—meaning they unconsciously come to understand them—*then perhaps you don't need official rules at all.*

It doesn't matter which option you choose. If handled carefully, the idea of classroom rules may indeed be a productive and fruitful discussion. However, if students can learn to work effectively with each other in a true learning community without the teacher ever needing to hem them in with a mandated set of rules, isn't that an even more empowering choice?

The way we handle rules is just one example of the many, many ways—large and small—of including students at higher levels of decision making. The following section gives you a host of other ideas for creating a self-perpetuating learning community in your Green Light classroom.

IMPLEMENTATION STRATEGIES

Tell Students Everything

One important way of including students is to share *every bit of information* with them. While this is contrary to the "need to know" information culture in many schools, telling your students the real reasons behind classroom decisions works on multiple levels. It demonstrates trust and respect, and it shows students you're all in this together.

So, if your principal hands you a stack of data indicating the areas of weakness for your class, don't hide it—share it! Tell your students you need their help in formulating a plan to overcome your class weaknesses. Share information about benchmarks and city goals. Explain how the test affects each student individually and the class as a whole. Talk openly about where the class needs to improve. Ask your students to set themselves a goal and choose learning activities to help meet it.

Often, when given all the available information (and the power to do something about it) your students will construct much-more-rigorous timelines and goals than you would have even considered.

For example: Let's say you get a reading-test score report back that states that the class is weak in vocabulary. You could create a sense of ownership by handling this situation as follows:

- **Include:** Hold a class meeting. Tell the students you need their help in an important matter. Perhaps ask them to pretend they are teachers. Share and explain the data.
- **Guide:** Give them a list of some suggested strategies that might work: flashcards, word of the day, practice tests, computer programs, word play.
- **Empower:** Let them choose which strategies to try in class. Students cannot complain about an activity when it is their idea! You can even let them choose how often to take quizzes to check progress. When they see the big picture, they understand why assessments are needed (Pressley et al., 2003).

Let Students Choose

There are plenty of opportunities in the course of a school day where you can provide opportunities for choice, without allowing your classroom to descend into anarchy. The key is to give choice within the context of what you, the teacher, wish to happen. For example, perhaps you're asking your students to draw a picture. You could let them choose whether they do so sitting at a desk or sitting on the floor. It doesn't matter *where* they do this task—as long as it gets done. Similarly, you want your students to review some material. You offer them the choice of making flashcards about the topic or making up a song about it or creating a collage. It doesn't matter *what* they do—as long as they learn the material.

The following eight suggestions all have this idea in common: They allow for student choice while progressing towards a lesson's aims (Tomlinson & McTighe, 2006). However small these choices seem, they can be extremely powerful when used consistently over time.

1. **Where to sit:** Let students sit where they choose, with the respectful note that they will be asked to choose a different seat if this one proves disruptive. Green Light classrooms constantly involve students moving from one table to another, so letting children choose their seats for the five minutes of that part of the lesson should be workable.

2. **Length of time to complete a task:** For example, give students a choice of 6, 8, or 10 minutes to complete a task. Does it really make or break the lesson? No, so give up that control. Let them feel that they are guiding the lesson. In the long run, you actually have *more* control because your students are following your plan to the end.

3. **Which partner to work with:** Let your students work with their friends once in a while. If they can choose to work with someone they like on occasion, they feel empowered and happy.

4. **The order of the lesson:** Share your lesson plan with your students. Is there anything in your plan that can be just as effective in a different order? If so, let them choose the order. Does it really matter if they do fraction games before the fraction sheet? You still get the same end result.

5. **Where to display work:** Let them decide on the decor of your classroom—the color of background paper, the position for different displays, the pattern of arranging artwork. Every time your students look up at the classroom walls, they will feel empowered by the fact that they chose their environment.

6. **What to read next:** Give your students responsibility for making sure they read right across the spectrum of genres during the year. Give them a list of what needs to be covered, and let them decide their own reading order.

7. **Which questions to answer:** Let your students choose 10 questions to answer out of 14. All of the questions assess the learning, so why not let them feel in control of which questions they want to answer?

8. **How to present projects:** Give your students the choice of presenting projects in a song, a play, a report, or a visual demonstration. As long as they get the key elements across, it doesn't matter how the information is presented.

Figure 1.1 shows a very specific example of how to let students choose their level and manner of participation. This spelling-assignment chart allows students to choose their preferred method of learning.

Figure 1.1 Spelling Menu

Name: _____ #: _____

SPELLING MENU

September 21–25

All work is due *Thursday*. The spelling test is *Thursday*.

5 Points	5 Points	5 Points
Create a *word web* for all of your words.	Create a *word pyramid* for all of your words.	Create *word toons* for all of your words.
10 Points	**10 Points** ***Must Do!***	**10 Points**
Create a poem using five of your words.	Sort your words, and draw a picture next to each word for the meaning.	List your words. Next to each word, write the part of speech (noun, verb, adjective, or adverb).
15 Points	**15 Points**	**15 Points**
Write a sentence with each spelling word. Your sentences must be at least five words long.	Write a paragraph using 10 of your words.	Find each spelling word in the dictionary, write the guide words and page number for each word.

Weekly Goal: 30 Points

3 Points: Parent signature on spelling menu (all 3 days).

Day	Number and Description of Activity	Points	Parent Sign Here
Monday	#___		
Tuesday	#___		
Wednesday	#___		

Let Students Talk

Once you introduce choice as a natural part of the school day, you'll find a new dynamic developing. You will talk less—and your students will talk more (Coleman, Rivkin, & Brown, 1997; Palinscar & Brown, 1984). This is a very important development and one you should welcome with great satisfaction. Remember, conversation leads to comprehension.

CONVERSATION LEADS TO COMPREHENSION

When students talk, they are highly engaged, able to pay attention for longer periods, and are actually processing the information. By contrast, when you talk, they can easily disengage and not be thinking about what you're saying. Perhaps even more important, the less you talk, the more your students own the learning process.

Be warned! If your current teaching style is to have long periods where you're the only one talking, this change will feel strange and possibly even a little uncomfortable. Some teachers actually start feeling guilty they are not teaching "properly" because they are no longer lecturing. Nothing could be further from the truth. As long as your classroom conversation remains on subject, your students will learn far more if they are the ones talking about the information.

Every time you have the instinct to present information to your students, see if you can find a way to allow them to talk about it. For example:

You Talk	They Talk
You tell the class they have weak spots in vocabulary.	You give students a graph showing average class scores in vocabulary on one curve and your class score on another. You ask them to discuss what this means.
You tell them about the activities you're going to use to improve their vocabulary.	You ask them to devise an action plan* to improve their vocabulary.
You tell them which activity they're going to start with.	You ask them to choose which activity they're going to do first.

*Most times, their plan will include all of the things you would have planned as well.

Another way to minimize how much you talk is to use nonverbal cues for instructions (see p. 95 in the Five-by-Five chapter).

Let Students Negotiate Change

From the very first day of school, send a clear message that you are open to suggestions and ideas (Jensen, 2008a). This means letting students know you value their input by constantly asking for and taking notes on their opinions and keeping the lines of communication open.

In particular, students should feel comfortable sharing their frustrations with you. If they come to you with a complaint or a dislike, try not to take it as a personal attack. They're simply telling you how they feel, and you should feel honored they trust you enough to share their feelings. If you respond negatively, they'll never trust you again.

Of course, you can't stop a teaching practice because a student doesn't like it, nor should complaining students be let off the hook. But, perhaps you can find another way of achieving the learning objective. Tell them the goal of the activity they dislike, and challenge them to come up with another way of meeting it. They will not only engage more enthusiastically with their alternative practice but will also have learned the art of compromise—another vital life lesson.

Case Study

The teacher required all students to complete short summaries about every chapter of their novel. After reading a chapter, they were required to stop, write down a few summary sentences, and then continue reading. This worked well for many readers in the class who needed help with comprehension, but Andrew—the most proficient reader—absolutely hated it. Andrew despised having to stop his flow of reading to write the summaries. He loved reading, finished chapters quickly, and couldn't understand the possible value of the summaries.

In a red light classroom, where students are taught never to question teaching practices, Andrew would have slowly lost his love of reading. Seething about the unfairness of it all, he would have scribbled down nonsense in his summaries, so he could quickly get back to the story, giving his teacher the impression he didn't understand the book. Eventually, he would have detached from the process of reading, hating school more with every passing day.

Fortunately, Andrew was in a Green Light classroom, where the teacher was open to students making suggestions. At the class meeting, Andrew tentatively suggested a different practice: Could he and other students have the option of writing a longer comprehension piece when they finished each whole book? His teacher readily agreed and Andrew, and a few of the other fast readers, joyfully stopped the hated chapter summaries and instead began turning in lengthy and enthusiastic book critiques.

Model Critical Thinking

All the practices in this chapter are fundamental building blocks for the skills required for critical thinking: gathering all the information, making decisions, discussing issues, coming up with solutions, and arguing a point. To help your students pull these building blocks together, the final piece of this strategy is modeling and celebrating critical thinking and problem solving (Mansilla & Gardner, 2008, p. 14–19).

As much as possible, model how you evaluate your own decisions, and discuss other choices you could have made that would have been more productive. This can be a constant theme in class meetings, reviewing class decisions and figuring out whether they were good ones and what you can learn from the outcomes.

Giving your students responsibility for learning not only improves test results; it also teaches higher-level thinking (perhaps the most important skill they will ever learn). Teach your students a fact and they pass a test. Teach them to think, and you equip them for succeeding in every area of life (Marzano, Pickering, & Pollock, 2001, p. 113).

Translations to Technology—Principle 1

Device	True Learning Communities: Students Taking Responsibility
Computer	Reflect your learning community in a class Web site—hosted on your school's intranet to ensure privacy—run by your students. Your Web site could include • Progress—showing full class test results (not individual results); • Profiles—students' own pages; • News—where students post family announcements; • Achievements—individual and class awards; • Blog spot—where students blog about their experiences in class; and • Library—photos and video clips of content-related activities to use for review before a test.
iPod	Allow students to choose the music for group activities.
Digital Camera	Just like pencils and paper, make your digital camera one of the basic resources available to your students at any time. Encourage them to use the camera whenever they choose—perhaps to help present a project. Take lots of digital photos of students every week. To support this, get your students into the habit of identifying "photo opportunities" when the class, a team, or an individual has achieved. Start every Monday morning with a PowerPoint show putting the best images to music (perhaps "Happy Together" by The Turtles or "Time of My Life" by Bill Medley and Jennifer Warnes). Be sure to include every child in the class. The photos will create a sense of joint achievement and also act as a review—your students will remember the content they were covering when the photo was taken.
Interactive Whiteboard	Use your interactive whiteboard to display the photos. Make a suggestion box on the interactive whiteboard to use during class meetings to encourage students to contribute.

KEY POINTS

- When classroom systems give students choice, teachers expend significantly less energy on classroom-management and discipline issues.
- When students are given responsibility for the learning process, they feel empowered and engage in the lessons at a higher level, increasing attention, understanding, and retention.
- Allowing students to make decisions—instead of telling them what to do—produces higher levels of engagement and ownership.
- Telling students everything demonstrates trust and respect, and it shows you're all in this together.
- The include-guide-empower sequence provides a concrete structure for allowing students to decide how to tackle important challenges.
- Frequent student-to-student conversations both improve comprehension and put students in control.

2 Optimum Learning Conditions

Creating Safety and Security

KINDNESS
is a LANGUAGE
we can All SPEAK

> *Breach the Dam!* *Students' motivation to be fully engaged in the learning process is often a direct reflection of their sense of safety and security in the classroom. Learning anything new is always risky, as the process inevitably requires occasional failure. How we handle unsuccessful efforts is critical to the students' future willingness to try the next time. What happens when they fail will encourage them to try, or deter them from trying, again. If failing is punitive or humiliating, they will cease to take the risk. But if they trust us to keep the classroom environment safe, they will try again and again until they succeed.*

OVERVIEW

We cannot learn without making mistakes. In fact, some of the most powerful learning comes from failure. Tell a child the stove is hot—they may or may not take in the lesson. But, they only need to fail to remember this warning once, and they will never touch the stove again.

Yet, in many red light classrooms, mistakes are the worst thing a student can make. For the brave soul making an effort, getting the answer wrong is often met with a scornful "No!" Written mistakes are highlighted in red and punctuated with disappointed crosses. Errors are sometimes even paraded in front of the class to the humiliation of the unfortunate child who made them.

The perpetrators of these mistakes certainly remember and learn from the way we handle error in our classrooms. They remember the negative emotions the moment generated—their anger, fear, or embarrassment—and they learn not to answer a question unless they're completely sure of the answer.

Clearly, this is not a supportive, constructive, or effective environment for learning. In a high-threat learning situation, where students feel at risk of looking stupid, the human desire to fit in means that few are willing to participate. Moreover, in an intimidating learning environment, students will constantly experience surges of anxiety or anger, which actually stop their brains from being receptive to learning—literally!

Fear and anger engage the amygdala, which activates the reptilian survival center in the brain. When the amygdala senses risk, it sends out an alarm message, and, before students have a chance to think, their system is flooded with adrenaline. Once that happens, learning is impossible. Your students are overwhelmed with the desire to freeze, flee, or fight, none of which is particularly useful in a learning context. While the reptilian survival center of the brain is engaged, students cannot access the brain's neocortex, which controls higher thinking, creativity, and intuition. In other words, they cannot think or learn effectively. They have hit what Stephen Krashen (1982) terms the *affective filter*. Krashen's hypothesis is that low motivation, low self-esteem, and debilitating anxiety can combine to raise the affective filter and form a mental block.

So, when a student makes a mistake, we have a choice: We can choose to turn it into a destructive moment of humiliation that stops the learning process, or we can make it a powerful learning experience that reinforces our content and encourages the student to continue learning (Drevets & Raichle, 1998, pp. 353–385; Jensen, 2008a, p. 48).

But, creating a secure environment is not just about the way we respond to individual mistakes. It's about the broader issue of trust. If your students trust you, they will be willing to take risks, and they will not be afraid to make the mistakes that will teach them the most valuable lessons.

Consider the spectrum of possibilities when a student gives an incorrect answer.

Worst Possible Case	Best Possible Case
The teacher is disappointed, dismissive, or downright rude about the answer. The teacher allows—perhaps even subtly encourages—the sniggers from other students. Clearly, this is bad for the humiliated student involved, but it also has a negative effect on the whole class. It may be happening to only *one* student, but *all* students are observing the moment and the teacher's reaction to it. Without realizing it, the teacher has primed the entire class to be wary of answering questions. Even while they are laughing at their classmate's discomfort, the other students are making a mental note: "That's not going to be *me!*"	The teacher, who understands that every response is an opportunity to build or destroy student confidence, treats even badly wrong answers with respect and encouragement. As a result, the student feels good about contributing and is motivated to try again. Meanwhile, the rest of the class is wishing they'd been the ones chosen to answer the question. Subliminally, the teacher has implanted some important messages about what happens in this classroom: *Contributing is rewarded by praise, every answer is respected, and participation feels good.*

How Safe Is Your Classroom?

You can gauge your classroom's *emotional safety* on a number of levels. If you want a quick straw poll, think about

- The *speed* with which your students engage;
- The *enthusiasm* with which they engage; and
- Their *willingness* to attempt new things.

Try asking for a volunteer for an unknown task. If you're facing a sea of enthusiastic hands, your classroom is secure. If only the two regular extraverts put their hands up, you may need to improve emotional safety in your classroom. This means looking at not just your responses, but what you permit to happen in the rest of the class.

Notice how it is not only the teacher who creates a sense of safety. Students are a huge part of generating and maintaining the feelings that permeate your classroom. While you, as the teacher, lead and set the tone, Green Light classrooms tap into the power of the student community to continually develop and enhance this important classroom dynamic. As a class, you must establish a culture where every student understands that students never make mistakes; they simply make discoveries.

If every classroom interaction were viewed through the lens of making discoveries, imagine what an incredible difference this would make in so many classrooms! Instead of making a mistake, a child has merely discovered one way that is not correct. Now the process can continue until a discovery is made that *is* the correct one! Handled appropriately, students will discover an important truth: Unsuccessful endeavors are not only OK but are also a natural and important part of learning.

Creating this sort of culture change in your classroom requires more than just acknowledging all student responses as valuable. You need to understand

- The specifics of *how* to handle incorrect responses;
- The specifics of how to handle *correct* responses;
- The *ongoing nature* of this dynamic; and
- The incredibly *fragile* nature of this dynamic.

If that sounds like a lot of trouble, here's the prize that makes paying this sort of attention worthwhile: student motivation.

Think about how often we discuss student motivation in education circles (Freeley & Hanzelka, 2009, p. 63–67). The primary focus is usually two parts:

- How can we *get* them engaged?
- How can we *keep* them engaged?

These questions seem to have a common underlying belief: that today's students *simply don't have any motivation!* Indeed, for these questions to be valid, we must assume that students have no interest in learning, that they bring no motivation with them to the classroom.

In a Green Light classroom, we start with an entirely different group of assumptions about today's students (Bartholomew, 2008, pp. 55–60). We believe that, in an emotionally safe classroom:

- Students *love* learning;
- Students *want* to learn;
- Students are actually *great* learners;
- Students have *plenty* of energy and enthusiasm for learning anything; and
- Students are *motivated* by the simple joy of being successful.

Consider this set of beliefs carefully. If these assumptions are even mildly true, then our entire approach to teaching must—absolutely must!—start from an entirely different viewpoint. Instead of finding ways to spark students' interest, we simply have to point them in the right direction and let their natural love of learning take over.

As teachers, then, our job becomes something different, and our role in the classroom takes on new meaning. No longer are we the pilot of the aircraft, burdened by the weight of all responsibility for the direction and focus of all learning on the journey. And no longer are students merely the passengers sitting passively (and uncomfortably) in their seats. Instead, we become the aircraft controller while our students fly the plane.

Our role still carries tremendous responsibility, yet in an entirely different way. We become the guide, overseeing the process, while students are deeply engaged and actively involved in the journey. Their natural energy and enthusiasm, channeled properly, charges the engines and propels the learning process forward.

The High-Five Principle of Optimum Learning Conditions creates a powerful domino effect: When students truly feel safe in the classroom, their natural motivation for learning is unleashed. And when the natural student motivation is given free rein, high levels of engagement follow naturally in its wake.

Engagement is the magic word for the highest levels of student learning. When students are emotionally engaged in the learning process, the true magic of the Green Light classroom happens. With only minimal effort on the part of the teacher, students dive into classroom activities, learn, and ultimately remember the lesson (Tate, 2003).

The following strategies give you specific ideas about how to make this happen: how to build a platform of confidence, security, and safety that encourages participation and allows natural motivation to power your classroom.

IMPLEMENTATION STRATEGIES

Do What You Say You Will Do

Like any other human relationship, students develop trust in their teacher by observing what they say—and then seeing whether they actually deliver on their promises. During the first week especially, but also throughout the year, you have to be very careful to tell your students the truth and do what you said you would do.

Here are some of the common phrases where teachers often fail to do this:

"We'll take a break in five minutes . . ."

"We'll stay here all day if we have to."

"I'll give you plenty of time to think about this."

"We won't continue until everyone has finished."

Be very conscious of—and deliberate about—what you are saying. Be careful of using glib phrases that may not hold up to reality. For example:

"This will be fun!"

"You'll enjoy this!"

"I have a great activity . . ."

"Here's something I know you'll all benefit from . . ."

Nothing will lose you trust more quickly than promising an enjoyable experience and delivering a boring one.

Never Say "No"!

As explained above, we need to honor and respect every child who makes an attempt—even when they get it wrong. If a child has given a "wrong" answer, here are some suggestions for responses instead of "no":

1. Yes, you're almost there; can I give you some think time?

2. Wow, I didn't think of it that way!

3. Thanks for your answer; now we're one step closer to what I was thinking.

4. Awesome! Talk with some people in your group to see if there is another answer out there.

5. You're thinking, and I like that; thanks for contributing.

When a child hears any of these responses instead of *no, wrong,* or *next,* they begin to trust you with their ideas because, suddenly, it's OK to get the answer wrong.

Encourage Learning From Mistakes

Deliberately promote the idea of learning from mistakes, using some of these novel techniques for discovery and review:

- Ask students for the incorrect answer (they still have to know the right one to give you this!).
- Ask students to put items in reverse order or carry out a procedure in the wrong order.
- Have a true-false quiz where the idea is to deliberately get the answers wrong.

- Tell stories about the mistakes Thomas Edison and Albert Einstein made, and the wonderful discoveries that were made as a result of these "mistakes."
- Tell stories about when *you* made mistakes in the past.
- When *you* make a mistake in the classroom, laugh at yourself, and be sure to call it a "learning opportunity."

Use Safe Language

When asking questions, make sure you don't scare off students by implying there's only one correct answer. Word your question to give them lots of room for error, or make it so they can't be wrong, or build your questions to point them to the answer.

Examples

1. "Who is the most important character in the book?"

Becomes . . .

"Who do you think is the most important character in the book?"

2. "What's the first step in solving this equation?"

Becomes a series of questions . . .

"What are some of the operations we might need to do to this equation?"

"What's our special phrase to help us remember the order of operations?"

"Which operation do you think we should do first?"

3. "What are the main points we have to remember?"

Becomes . . .

"If you were teaching this to someone, what are some of the things you'd want them to remember?"

4. "What is the author's purpose?"

Becomes . . .

"If you were the author, what are some possible reasons you would have for writing this piece?"

Create Powerful Rituals

The goal in a Green Light classroom is for students to walk in saying to themselves, "I know what's going to happen, and I know how to participate." This is why we establish the routines you'll find on pages 92–94 in the Five-by-Five chapter. Once you've established these important rituals, your students will know what to do when each activity song comes on, what your silent cues mean, and how to celebrate their own and each other's success. This creates a powerful sense of belonging and comfort.

Dramatics Confirm Safety

When students begin to feel truly safe (Jensen, 2009, p. 3; Wolfe, 2001), you can confirm and support this level of safety by being more dramatic and acting out lessons—something students would never do if they were in fear of embarrassment or ridicule.

Here are some ways to add more dramatic spice to your classrooms:

- Create a daily game show to review concepts. Ham it up! Ask one student to speak in a booming voice like a host, and choose a few students as excited contestants. When students "win" by answering the questions, make up imaginary grand prizes.
- After each lesson, ask students to interview each other about what they learned in the lesson. This is a great wrap-up activity. Using a pencil as a microphone, demonstrate with great exaggeration, "Hello this is your teacher from Channel 11 news, and I have the famous student Mike here to answer a few questions. Tell me, Mike, what did you learn today about the life cycle of a frog?"
- As much as possible, bring dress-up activities into your classroom. If you teach history, for example, use it as an opportunity for grand plays and reenactments.
- Turn boring grammar and editing lessons into a chance to become a doctor. Tell your students they are going to diagnose and treat "sick" paragraphs. Let them dress up in lab coats and stethoscopes to get them excited about fixing that paragraph. For more details on this idea, see "Lesson Set 1: The Editing Doctors" in Chapter 7 (pp. 124–127).

Laugh All the Time

Nothing banishes anxiety like laughter: It's a great stress reliever, triggering positive emotions and a tremendous feeling of well being (Tate, 2003, p. 38; Sousa, 2001). So find opportunities for your class to laugh together whenever you can—with you leading the way.

- Use silly voices and accents—this always descends into laughter.
- Tell a funny story to begin a lesson.
- Make daily routines fun: Ask students to go pick up a book while moving like their favorite animal, or ask them to stick their tongue out if they've found the right page.
- Playfully give them funny cues like "Put your finger *up* . . . I mean *on* your nose when ready." Act as if you genuinely made a slip up.
- Involve volunteer students in gross sentences when teaching grammar. For example, "Bobby made slime cookies and ate them."
- Use weird, creative, or even made-up words to make your students laugh!

Before you dismiss the above suggestions as inappropriate or unprofessional, please remember that, like every strategy in this book, they have a *purpose*. Their purpose is to make your students laugh together, because there is nothing more powerful to bind a group or create a safe emotional environment than *shared laughter*. So, if you're thinking some of the ideas seem a bit "corny," that's because . . . they are! They're pitched at the humor level of the kids in your classroom! However, while they are deliberately designed to create moments of levity, their purpose is incredibly serious and important. It's about getting your students to the optimal emotional state for learning. Thus, despite the seemingly silly nature of the ideas, they support an extremely professional and worthy goal.

Translations to Technology—Principle 2

Device	Optimum Learning Conditions: Creating Safety and Security
Computer	Computers offer us an important means of allowing students to make mistakes privately. For example: • Create or use ready-made self-checking quizzes (try www.quia.com) so students can practice for a big test in a nonthreatening way. Their score is not recorded; they can make mistakes and move on. • Allow students to e-mail you their first draft, and send them your suggestions in confidence—then post their corrected final version on the interactive whiteboard or Web site. • Use anonymous polls to gain class opinions.
iPod	Use music during small-group discussions as a "cover" under which less-confident students can speak, safe in the knowledge that others can't overhear them.

Device	Optimum Learning Conditions: Creating Safety and Security
Interactive Whiteboard	Be careful with interactive whiteboard activities that pit student against student or that create a high-threat situation: • Always allow the class to coach the student working at the board. This will encourage less-confident learners to happily stand in front of the class, knowing their peers will be helping them out, not watching and laughing at their mistakes. • When activities are not timed, let students show you on paper what they think the answer is before touching it on the interactive whiteboard. Give them a visual cue, like a thumbs up, that they are about to show the class a correct answer.
Digital Camera	Take short video clips whenever students act out content. Your students will be more highly motivated to participate, and the clips will be excellent review material.

KEY POINTS

- Mistakes are a natural, normal, and necessary part of the learning process.
- Every student response, whether right or wrong, is an opportunity to either build—or destroy—student confidence.
- What the teacher says and does when a student makes a mistake has an enormous impact on the student's reaction, as well as affecting future student efforts.
- The *willingness* to answer questions, the *speed* with which answers are given, and the *enthusiasm* with which they are delivered are all significant indicators of the emotional safety level of the classroom.
- In a truly effective learning environment, students never make *mistakes;* they simply make *discoveries.*
- When students truly feel safe in the classroom, their natural motivation for learning is unleashed.
- When the natural student motivation is given free rein, high levels of engagement follow naturally in its wake.
- Trust can be developed with students by always doing what you say you will do.
- Classroom rituals are fundamental to creating a sense of safety and security.
- Laughter brings joy to the learning process, strengthens the bond between teacher and student, and helps encode powerful memories of the content.

3 Teaching to the Moment

Working Within Their *World*

Inspire
the creative genius
in kids and create
life-long learners

Breach the Dam! *Lesson plans are, essentially, hallucinations. While they may be helpful in creating a structure from which to launch a successful lesson, we must remember they are purely theoretical concepts. As soon as class begins, real teachers start making real adjustments—for real students. If your lesson plan is working—and working well—rock on! If not, don't let the lesson plan hold you back—adjust the approach for what's real to your students, what's on their minds, and follow the raging torrent of their enthusiasm for what naturally interests them.*

IT'S SO LOVELY....

OVERVIEW

In many ways, a good classroom is a delicate balancing act, a show worthy of the center ring in any circus. It requires in-the-moment finesse, flair, and panache. In one hand, we juggle the classroom structures that are so important to success: rituals, sequences, objectives, and goals. In the other hand, we juggle the true keys to achieving educational outcomes: flexibility, creativity, and adaptability. It is only the proper blend of both hands working together that creates a successful Green Light classroom.

Structure is critical in many aspects of life. A magnificent building is only possible because it has been built around a solid design of columns and crossbeams. Popular TV shows have clearly established, familiar formats that audiences recognize and are comfortable with. Sporting events function with clearly established guidelines, and the stars are those who excel creatively within these boundaries. Even musical improvisation only works because the players first agree on a given key and know the chord structures that make the improvised sound appealing. Structure not only underlies form and function but art and beauty as well—it is essential to the way our world works.

Similarly, structure is critical in the learning process. Students need the consistency and comfort of firmly established classroom rituals. Teachers need clarity in knowing what students need to learn, within what timeframe. Equally important, we need a clear sense of direction, focus, and purpose to guide a lesson towards our intended learning goal.

However, structure in the learning process, in and of itself, can all too quickly become a trap that inhibits and restricts learning. By rigidly adhering to a lesson plan, we lose the opportunity to teach "in the moment." In other words, we miss the moments where something has sparked the interest of the class because our lesson plan didn't see it coming. Here are some of the most common moments that lesson plans don't allow for.

The Left-Field Question

A student makes a comment only tangentially related to your lesson, but it sparks interest with many others in the class.

- Red light teachers think, "I don't have time to go down that path—we'll get too far off course, and we'll run out of time." They shut down the student, brush off the comment, and find a way to get back on the "right" track. The class goes back to gazing out of the window.

- Green Light teachers think, "Excellent, I had never thought it that way! I wonder how I can use that remark to spur the lesson forward?" They answer the question, which sparks more interest from the reengaged class, eventually bringing the discussion back to join up with the original content. The lesson charges forward with everyone participating.

This is not to say that all unusual comments or bizarre off-the-wall student remarks will open a floodgate of ideas every time they are uttered in the classroom—not at all! However, the key is to keep our thinking open—to allow for the possibility of spontaneous creativity. If even only a few questions open new doors within a lesson, the advantages are enormous. And not just in terms of this particular lesson. When your students see you responding in the moment like this (respecting what they're interested in) they feel a part of the classroom community. These students will be more readily engaged in future lessons, making the teaching process easier and more productive next time.

The Light-Bulb Moment

There is a moment in every lesson plan where we assume our students have "got it"—after which we move on to practice and application. The problem is that most groups of students get it sooner—or later—than our plan allows for. As soon as students get it, they want to try it out! If we plow on, giving all the examples we planned, long after the light has switched on, students will lose the moment and tune out. Then, when we finally do allow them to practice, their energy will be down. Equally, if we throw them into practice before they are ready, they will fail—potentially putting them off the activity forever.

- Red light teachers ignore lightbulb moments and relentlessly make students sit through unnecessary examples. They also fail to notice when the class has just not got it and put them through the pain of unnecessary failure.
- Green Light teachers recognize when the class has got it early, ditching vast quantities of plans and immediately putting the eureka moment to good and practical use. They also check to make sure the class is ready to apply the information and have back-up plans to get across material in a different way if the original lesson plan fails.

The Hijack Moment

Before you start the lesson, the class is already buzzing because a student has announced or brought in something exciting. You have a really good frame planned for your lesson, which normally works well.

- Red light teachers plow on with their original lesson plan, wondering why it's just not sparking the same levels of interest as usual and why discipline is particularly difficult this morning.
- Green Light teachers throw out their planned frame and use the new source of excitement as a jumping-off point for the lesson, harnessing the buzz in the room and using it to fuel interest in the lesson.

The New Fad

Imagine that perhaps last year, with considerable effort, you developed an excellent frame for this lesson based on the latest craze sweeping your class. However, you haven't heard anything about this craze for a while, nor have you heard your students talking about it.

- Red light teachers use the latest craze frame anyway (Hey, it took hours to develop!) and wonder why students are rolling their eyes and refusing point blank to answer any questions.
- Green Light teachers, who keep in touch with student interests, know that craze is now so uncool that even mentioning the name brings social death to the person in question (pet rocks, mood rings, or Tamagotchi, anyone?). They build a new frame based on any *new* craze that is currently sparking their students' interest. This starts the lesson off with a burst of energy as students excitedly show off their knowledge of this current trend, and it engages their interest in the lesson.

The issue is that trends come and go with astonishing rapidity. A popular game can be in one day and totally out the next. We need to do our best to keep up with these passing trends and constantly reframe our lesson plans to ensure our teaching remains in our students' world.

In all of these situations, the key is to remember that a prepared lesson is only an abstract construct, a theoretical design—basically, just an idea. No matter how carefully thought out in advance, it will never be as good as your ability to respond to what is actually happening in the moment. Also, as illustrated in the final example, a lesson plan is never "done"; it will always need refreshing to ensure its frame is relevant to your students.

Ironically, it is often the lessons we think out *most carefully* that are at the most risk. As teachers, we become so deeply invested in our plan, so attached to it, that we are unwilling to allow for even minimal change (regardless of the effect it may be producing in the moment). When we are convinced a lesson plan will be successful, we become blinded to our students' level of responsiveness and engagement. Green Light teachers stay alert to the siren call of this seductive yet destructive lure and make careful choices that allow them to deliver the most effective and powerful lesson—in the moment.

Let's be clear: Planning a lesson is not a bad thing. In fact, the opposite is true. Every lesson should be carefully constructed and thought through in advance. A carefully thought-out lesson can often dictate the success or failure of a lesson. At the same time, we need to remember the words of Dwight D. Eisenhower, who said,

"Plans are nothing; planning is everything." (BrainyQuote, 2010)

Creating a lesson plan is a highly valuable endeavor. However, we must remember the plan is *not real*. When we confuse a plan formed in advance with the reality of a situation in the present, we become unable to make appropriate adjustments. Consider the popular adage *the map is not the territory,* or its translation to teaching: *The lesson plan is not the lesson.*

Instead, the lesson is a very real, vibrant, exciting creation, pulsating with a life and vitality of its own. For Green Light teachers, this is exciting news! It means that every day is different, every class is distinctive, and every lesson is unique. Indeed, every opportunity to teach becomes a *new chance for us to learn something too!* What will today bring? What new and fascinating questions will students ask? What unexpected changes in direction will a lesson take? At a fundamental level, it is this very state of fascination *on the part of the teacher* that most clearly distinguishes red and Green Light classrooms.

You may feel this is all laboring a fairly simple point: Of course good teachers always adjust the lesson to meet the needs of their students! Or do they? Many dedicated teachers actually teach exactly the same lesson plans year in, year out. And, even those who believe they adapt to the moment are surprised when they discover *how* Green Light teachers make adjustments, by what degree and to what extent.

Teachers' Thoughts About Adapting a Lesson Plan	
Red Light Focus	**Green Light Focus**
What changes are needed so I can keep students tucked in, and get them back on track with the lesson plan?	*What are the students truly interested in today, and how can I use their own excitement and energy to propel them towards better learning the material? How can I teach using what's real to them?*

The key, then, is to ask where we are putting our focus—on the *plan*, or on the *students*.

If we only focus on the plan, both students *and* the teacher pay a high price. Students become bored and disengaged, leading to discipline problems for the teacher to manage. In contrast, moving our focus to our students creates the opposite effect. Students are interested, and therefore they become more interesting to the teacher. When our awareness switches from enforcing the boundaries of the lesson to uncovering what's real for the students, it opens up a new world of teaching possibilities. The same energy we might previously expend (waste?) on control is now free to be used to ponder new and creative ways of teaching the same idea.

Does it take energy, determination, and focus to remain tuned into what's real for the students and make adjustments to a lesson accordingly? Yes, it absolutely does. But keep in mind the two penalties of the red light approach: First, it takes a high level of energy to continually reinforce the boundaries of a preestablished lesson plan; and second, this energy *must all come from you, the teacher!*

But, look at what happens when you teach to what's real for your students. You surf the moment and ride the wave of interest! The metaphor of the bursting dam is a pervasive aspect of this book, and it applies in this situation as well. When we tap into discussions that are relevant to our students, we set free a torrent of natural energy, enthusiasm, and curiosity. As the teacher, all we truly need to do is ride this energetic wave of interest and gently channel it towards our intended objective. We do that by maintaining a flexible, creative, open mindset and doing our best to adapt our lesson in the moment to what's real to our students on *that* day and in *that* moment.

RIDE
THE
WAVE

Thus, lesson plans should not be *planned* but only *outlined*. They should have strong bones, like a skeleton, but the meat should be filled in according to your students' interest in the lesson and how it unfolds in the moment.

The keys to success with this principle are twofold. First, truly understand the difference between what is real to our students—what they are interested in, fascinating by, or passionate about—versus what *we think* should be important to them. Second, keep an open mind and deliberately adapt our lesson plans to hook into what's real for our students.

IMPLEMENTATION STRATEGIES

Use Tangential Questions

Even totally left-field comments can help you unlock student interest in a lesson. Try to use the characters or the facts your students introduce and include them in the lesson. Here are some examples:

Subject	Question/Comment	Green Light Response
History	Pete: "My Dad went to Washington, D.C., last year on business."	"Wow, how interesting! OK, let's imagine Pete's Dad has a time machine. If he goes back to November 6, 1860—and lands in the White House gardens—do you know which president he'd see being elected that day?"
Science	Mary: "My brother's socks are so smelly, they attract flies!"	"Well, class let's help Mary test what's happening. How could she conduct an experiment to see how many flies his socks attract? What is the question? How many flies can Mary's brother's socks attract in one hour? Does anyone have a hypothesis?"
Reading	David: "I saw the greatest movie ever last night!"	"David, who were the characters in the movie? What was the main problem in the story? If we were to make the movie into a book, what would the climax be? Let's look at other popular movies. Find the conflict in . . ."
Math	Suki: "My big sister has tickets to see Pink—she's going with her friends!"	"How cool! Raise your hand if you'd like to go to Pink too! Me too! I wonder how much that would cost. Suki, do you know how much the tickets cost? . . . OK, so $100 times 25—that's a hard sum? But, there's an easy trick to work it out. Shall I show you how . . . ?"
Writing	Angela: "I love to paint with watercolors!"	"How many of you love to paint? Most of you use a paintbrush, right? Did you know that you can paint with other things, like words! Let's try to paint a beautiful scene with just words."

Spot the Lightbulb Moment

It's vital to introduce *practice* the moment the class is ready to apply any new concept or activity. But how can you tell? Here are some ideas to help you gauge this moment.

- **I got it!:** At the beginning of the year, you will establish a number of silent cues (see pp. 98–100). One of these is an extremely helpful student cue that means "I got it!" If you encourage your students to use this cue, you may never again have to guess when the lightbulb moment occurs—your students will tell you!
- **Traffic lights:** If you want to obtain more information on progress, give your students three flash cards, colored red, yellow, and green. Explain that these are for them to tell you their level of understanding (red = "I don't understand," yellow = "I'm getting there," green = "I got it!"). Tell them that in every lesson they will look to move from red to green. Every so often, have a "check-in" moment, where students hold up the card that best explains their understanding. Do this right at the beginning—to check if any students already learned this, but also to acknowledge it's OK *not* to know something. When you get mostly green cards, you'll know it's time to practice.
- **Dropping off:** If students start fidgeting or looking around, you've lost them. This may be because they got it, or they may have just reached the end of their ability to concentrate. Either way, it's time to do something different. Throw them into a simple application or discussion of your content. If they've got it, this will tell you quickly, and you can move on to the practice stage of your lesson. If not, it will give them a break and you time to figure out how to reengage the class.
- **Quiet rumbles:** If you hear the mumbling of students to each other while delivering a lesson, stop and find out what they think is so much more important than the lesson at hand. Find out what is occupying their interest, and incorporate it in the lesson. Or, just let them get out what they wanted to say, and move on. Once the issue has been addressed, they are more likely to pay attention.
- **Let them decide:** If you think most of the class has got it, give them a choice: Students who are comfortable with the material can find a partner and start practicing; everyone else can join you in the class meeting place to talk more about it. You'll soon get a handle on the level of understanding in your classroom.

Tune In

The best—and easiest—thing a Green Light teacher can do to follow this High-Five principle of Teaching to the Moment is to simply "tune in" to the students. A tuned-in teacher knows what will grab the interest of the students and uses it to keep them motivated and learning. Here are some ways of becoming a well-tuned-in teacher.

- Always chat with students before and after class, especially about things that are going on in their lives beyond the classroom.
- Note the current trends, songs, artists, fashions, and fads they are talking about.
- Watch students carefully while they are at play, inside or outside, and in the lunchroom.
- Give opportunities for student choice, and watch how many choose certain options. This is another strong indicator of what will and won't work in your lesson plan.

Tuning in also helps you identify issues that might otherwise derail your lessons. You'll hear about rumors, worries, or concerns, and you will have the chance to deal with them before they prevent students from engaging with the learning process. For example, imagine the classroom is buzzing with a rumor that the school picnic has been cancelled. Your students are upset and angry. There's no point launching into your lesson plan—your students are in no state to learn. So, call a quick class meeting immediately, and either put the rumor to rest, or if it's true, let your students talk about their disappointment and perhaps figure out an alternative treat. Then, when emotions are calmer, you can begin teaching to a more receptive audience.

If you don't know what students' interests are, *ask them.* Their answers will provide ample suggestions for ways to teach certain topics, new lessons you could offer, and—most important—show that you care. Here are some even more specific ways to keep tabs on student interests and the way they really feel about your lessons:

- **First-day survey:** Consider giving your students a survey on the first day of school, allowing them to voice their opinions about the teacher they had the previous year. You may find out something important that could inform your decisions on a broad level for the entire upcoming year. For example, perhaps most students hated when the overhead projector was used—then don't use it! Or perhaps a majority of them hated the use of the Socratic approach to asking questions. If so, you've just learned something important (even though the idea may be a valid approach to teaching) what's real to them is that it triggers a negative reaction. You'll need to use a different method of asking questions to avoid getting a similar response. Learning as much as you can from the very beginning gives you a huge advantage.

- **Monday class meetings:** Every Monday, allow students to share their weekend activities with the class. You will quickly learn your students' priorities. Weekend narratives also provide a peek into student home life. For example: Mrs. Sherrer could not get her 10-year-old boys interested in reading nonfiction. She tried everything. When she started holding class meetings, she quickly learned that the boys all liked football. When she presented them with NFL articles on their favorite players, the boys loved learning to read nonfiction. Through these meetings, she also learned that one boy's father was no longer around, something the boy's mother had failed to mention. She quickly set him up with a male mentor, and he got back on the right track in learning to read.

- **Morning door dialogue:** General conversation in the morning, before class starts, is always an important way to gather information about your students. However, consider some days actually greeting students at the door and asking them how their morning is going (Hollas, 2005, p. 81). Some may stop and let you know that a pet just died, their grandma is ill, or that it's their sister's birthday. This is all valuable information to set the tone for the day. They may also tell you that they are excited about something like a sporting event. This could give you lesson ideas. For example: If a student tells you that she is excited about going to a professional baseball game later in the day, you could structure the math lesson around baseball—how many miles they have to drive from their house to the stadium, the scores, or pitching averages.

- **Actively seek feedback:** If you're waiting with your students for the final bell to ring, start a casual conversation about what did and didn't work in the lessons today. You might pose the question, "Tell me, if you could change one thing about today's lesson and do it over again, what would it be?" You might be surprised by what they did and didn't like, and you'll be able to adapt tomorrow's lessons based on real insight—not guess work.

- **Ask about details:** "Hey what does that name mean on your shirt?" Most students will be delighted to explain about their favorite brands. The same applies to video games and gadgets. Just *ask,* and usually you will get an enthusiastic response. Later, you can use this information in your lessons. For example, say Mr. Thompson asked young Jenny why she had a big H on her shirt. She explained that it stood for the new designer, Huli, who comes from Hawaii. Mr. T then realized that most of the female students were wearing similar shirts (something he never paid attention to). Immediately, Mr. T can make up some math word problems using Huli's travel route from Hawaii to New York fashion shows, using model height—and on and on! Mr. T can be certain that all of the girls paid attention in math class that day.

Case Study

Mr. Johnson's English objective for the day is for students to master adverbs. He knows that he needs to have an introduction, student practice, and a closing that checks for understanding. Through the class meeting, Mr. J discovered that most of the students in the class are loyal fans of the local basketball team. Mr. J plays a video replay of parts of the game. He asks, "How did the star player jump?" (Students reply with *quickly, gracefully,* etc.) Students are so excited about the video, they don't even realize they are making up sentences with adverbs and identifying them, meeting the objective of the day. Later, when Mr. J checked for understanding, they all showed a proficient knowledge because they were interested.

The more you know about your students' world beyond the walls of your classroom (and the walls of the school building) the easier it will be to connect with them, and the easier it will be to make the appropriate adjustments to your lessons. Once you tune in to the world of your students, you'll be able to create interest-appropriate lessons, teach to the moment, and work within their world.

Translations to Technology—Principle 3

Device	Teaching to the Moment: Working Within Their World
Computer	The rise of the Internet is moving the focus of education from knowing "things" to knowing "how." Use unusual questions to teach your students Internet research skills. If a student raises a general knowledge question the class can't answer, allow them to immediately Google the answer. Use the moment to teach the class how to search—give them a quick dos-and-don'ts overview, and ask for search-word suggestions.
iPod	The Monday class meeting reveals a new song is highly popular. Download the song in the next break, and surprise your students as a special reward.
Digital Camera and Interactive Whiteboard	When a student brings in something for show and tell, take a digital photograph, and upload it immediately onto the interactive whiteboard. The student will love seeing his toy or artifact projected for all the class to see—magnifying his sense of importance.

KEY POINTS

- Lesson plans are guidelines only, and they should be primarily used as an outline for teaching a dynamic lesson . . . *in the moment.*
- Excessive structure in the learning process can become a trap that inhibits and restricts learning.
- Any current source of student excitement is a possible jumping-off point for a lesson to harness the buzz in the room and channel it to fuel interest in the topic.
- When our awareness switches from enforcing the boundaries of the lesson to uncovering what's real for the students, it opens up a new world of teaching possibilities.
- When we tap into discussions that are relevant to our students, we set free a torrent of natural energy, enthusiasm, and curiosity.
- Tuning into what is important to your students helps you identify issues that might otherwise work subconsciously to undermine a lesson.
- It's vital to introduce *practice* the moment the class is ready to apply any new concept or activity.
- The more you know about your students' world beyond the walls of your classroom (and the walls of the school building) the easier it will be to connect with them and to make appropriate adjustments to your lessons.

4 Learning Beyond Listening

Linking Action and Understanding

YOUR I CAN IS MORE IMPORTANT THAN YOUR I.Q.

Breach the Dam! Adding movement to lessons brings them to life and helps students remember information better. Instead of trying to contain our students' natural liveliness, by battling to make them sit still and be quiet while the teacher talks, we can carefully guide the instinctive flow of children's need to move to draw them further and deeper into the learning process.

OVERVIEW

One of the most striking things about a Green Light classroom is its physicality. In a red light classroom, the primary teaching method remains "lecture and listen"; in a Green Light classroom, it is movement. You can tell a Green Light classroom immediately because students are constantly active: running to touch the right answer on the board; moving their bodies in response to questions; always, in some way, being physically involved in the teaching process. Often, students are on their feet for the vast majority of the lesson (Zmuda, 2008, pp. 38–42).

The result is an extraordinary level of engagement and focus from all students. If you actively encourage your students to move, they can't help but participate. But, the benefit of physical involvement goes beyond better engagement; it also helps students to grasp new material rapidly and easily commit information to memory in a surprisingly short period of time.

Why? Because you are harnessing the energy that works *against* teachers in a traditional classroom and directing it to enhance engagement, understanding, and recall. In a traditional learning setting, students devote a great deal of energy to simply keeping focused and paying attention. Instead, you can take this energy—the fidgeting and the foot tapping and the desperate need to move that nearly all primary students bring into our classrooms—and use it to *fuel* the learning process.

This is not to say listening is not important. Listening is certainly a skill all students need to develop. Listening for understanding during lessons, listening for directions during activities, and listening to the input of peers during discussions are all critical and necessary aspects of the learning process. However, lecture and listen as the *primary* means of teaching is simply *not* a viable method of instruction for working with today's primary students. While teaching by talking is certainly still a valid option for some aspects of learning, we should only use it as a last resort: when no other method is possible. Instead, we should take every opportunity to get our students up and moving while they learn.

The most obvious benefit of engaging primary students physically is that it makes classroom management much easier. Students who can't concentrate during lecture-and-listen sessions tend to act out. Get them moving, and their active bodies keep their minds engaged with the lesson, not their daydreams (Knecht et al., 2004, pp. 20–26).

But, the benefits go much deeper. Learning by *doing* is perhaps the single most effective way to help primary students understand and remember a new concept. If students encode a central lesson concept through muscle memory, the learning is deep and lasting.

Kinesthetic learning has always been very powerful for younger students; but today, the increasing use of interactive electronic games is making the need for movement in the learning environment even more important. In 2008, despite the recession, software sales in the U.S. gaming market grew by 26%. As more and more kids are routinely exposed to the immersive, high-stimulation environments created by games like Wii and Xbox, their learning styles are changing. Their attention spans contract, their ability to sit still reduces, and their preference for experiential learning becomes more pronounced.

> *Physical engagement used to be a "nice to have." Now it's absolutely essential if we want to keep elementary students engaged.*

We may not be able to recreate the complete attention-grabbing technological experience in our classrooms, but we can replicate the learning style of interactive games: physical engagement, trial and error, and learning by doing. If we base our lessons on these principles—instead of listen and learn—we trigger numerous positive effects:

- More engaged students, leading to less distractions and discipline issues
- The release of energy during the movement, so students are better able to focus during the next section if they need to be seated
- More students learning the lesson faster
- Less need to reteach content at a later time
- A more lively, engaging classroom environment
- Students remembering key content more easily

So, how do we link action with learning? As the following apparently simple, yet highly effective, examples demonstrate, the key is to deliberately build movement into every aspect of your classroom—to take every single possible opportunity to fuel the learning process by harnessing your students' energy (Van Praag, Christie, Sejnowski, & Gage, 1999, pp. 13427–13431).

IMPLEMENTATION STRATEGIES

Ask for Movement in the Response

A simple means of making your lessons more active is to make movement a part of any choral response. This keeps your students engaged by allowing them to include their need to move as a legitimate part of your lesson, and you actually end up with better quality responses and important opportunities to check learning progress.

- **Students give physical, visible gestures as responses:** Rather than asking students for a vocal answer to your questions, ask them for a physical response. For example, you might say, "Raise your hand if . . ." or, "Nod your head if . . ." or, "When you have finished, hold your thumb in the air." This gives you a valuable "check for understanding" moment—it's much easier to pick out kids who don't move than kids who don't answer. It also allows the students to link action to their understanding.
- **Students give a *unique* physical gesture:** Rather than asking your students to respond with a simple physical gesture, try introducing an unusual movement. You might ask them to, "Put your thumb on your nose when you have finished" or, "Put both elbows on your knees when you're ready." The rationale for this is that younger students enjoy doing something unusual or odd. Often, they giggle when making the gesture, a sure sign they're completely engaged with the moment. Also, when they realize they will get to do something fun or silly when they have accomplished a task, it often drives them to complete the task more rapidly.
- **Students use a physical object when responding:** You can have a lot of fun mixing your responses up. Rather than making a gesture, try asking your students to move an object. You might say, "When you have finished, place your book on your head" or, "If you're ready, hold you pencil high in the air" or, "If you've found page 58, hold your text book out in front of you."
- **Students stand up:** If students are sitting, another form of this technique is to ask them to stand up if they know the answer to a question. For example: "If you now know the three branches of government, stand up!" or, "If you can remember the names of the seven continents, stand up!"
- **Students move their whole body:** If your students are already standing, ask for a response that requires moving their entire body. You might say, "I'm going to list some jobs—when I say one that is in the *legislative* branch of the government, hop on one leg." Of course, this doesn't tell you which students know the answer. One

student will start hopping, and everyone will quickly follow suit. But, the point is, the students who didn't know the answer before will know it *now*, because they will remember when they hopped.

Use Various Locations for Learning

Establish different locations in your classroom for different types of learning. This builds in active engagement as a natural by-product of your lesson as students move from location to location. Another benefit is that, once your students know a particular type of instruction will ensue in a certain location, when asked to move to that location, they will automatically start to prepare for that type of instruction. When students instinctively know what is coming, they feel safe and comfortable. At a subtle level, they take ownership of the next segment of the lesson.

- **Lessons often start with students sitting on the floor:** When you're planning a "location lesson," *start* with students sitting on the floor clustered around you. This is a good position from which to explain what they'll be doing. Then, when they stand up to go to the various stations around the room, the act of simply standing up from the floor works as a physical engager. Standing up from the floor works much better than standing up from being seated in a chair because it takes more energy.
- **Students move to different stations:** The basic idea of a location lesson is to avoid students completing activity after activity while seated at their desks. Instead, you simply put each aspect of the activity at a separate station in various places around the room. The physical act of moving to a new station will kick start attention levels as students move to a new task.
- **Lessons often end with students sitting on the floor:** Try to end the lesson with all your students seated back on the floor again. This return to the original physical location acts as a trigger, helping to remind students what you set out to learn about in the lesson. Now, you can talk about what they've learned from the activities at the various locations. Remember to point to the location where they learned a particular piece of content when you discuss it. This will trigger the memory of them standing at that station, helping them to contribute to the discussion.

Involve Students Physically in the Learning Process

So far, we've talked about building movement into our teaching strategies. And you'll get an even more powerful learning outcome if you can link movement directly to your content—your students will learn faster and remember longer. This is because movement engages our *muscle* or *procedural memory*—literally a memory learned through movement. Procedural memory is one of the most lasting forms; meaning, if we learn a task by physically doing it, it tends to stay with us for a long time. Current research suggests this may be because muscle movement triggers glucose production and engages far more neurons than simple cognitive tasks such as adding. Thus, literally acting out information increases the chances of your students recalling your lesson.

It's important to get into the habit of looking at every piece of core content and, in some creative way, linking it to action in the learning process. For example:

- **Students often run to point at the board, or a map:** Occasionally, let students run up and touch the board at appropriate moments. You can use this basic idea in a variety of ways, in many different lessons. For example, when learning about sentence construction, ask students to run up and touch the noun, the adjective, or the verb. Or, when teaching geography, ask them to run up and touch a location, such as a city or a mountain range. When students learn this way, they link the action to the visual information and store it more effectively in their long-term memory.

- **Students physically indicate a choice by moving to the *sides* of the room:** When asking students to express how strongly they agree or disagree with a subject, try using the sides of the room to indicate choice. For example, you might use this technique by saying, "Let's think about the Boston Tea Party and what the colonists did. If you think those people did the *right* thing, stand over on this side of the room. If you think they did the wrong thing, stand over on this side of the room. If you're not sure, you can stand in the middle." You can use this idea in multiple ways, allowing students to express their opinions about different things, while using movement. It also visually allows them to quickly and easily see what other students are thinking. The other great benefit is that *every* student joins in every time, something that rarely happens with purely verbal responses. It allows even those shy or slow students—those who differentiated instruction pundits refer to as "early readiness" students—who never raise their hand, to participate and have an opinion.

- **Students physically indicate a choice by moving to the *corners* of the room:** For another version of the above strategy, use the corners of the room. For example: "If you believe that summer is the best season, go this corner; if you think winter is the best, go to that corner."

- **Use a grid on the floor of the classroom to teach math:** You can add movement to a math lesson with a floor-size math grid. The simplest way to create one is by using masking tape to draw a 10′ × 10′ square grid on the floor—a "100 square." The math grid stays on the floor of your classroom all the time, so you can use it to physically do math problems whenever possible. For example, you might ask every student to run and stand on a number. Then, you can call out a problem—you might say, "Subtract 12 from that number, and stand on the answer!" Or, "Triple that number, and stand on the answer!" Even students who hate math *love* doing this, as they move their bodies to demonstrate their knowledge. They also find it easier to grasp math concepts. The muscle memories developed by the grid, and the highly visual representation of each math problem, seem to create lightbulb moments for students who flounder when faced with math worksheets. Another major advantage for less-confident mathematicians, the grid reduces the threat involved in making mistakes. A wrong sum in their math textbook turns into a permanent record of their error; whereas standing on the wrong square is an "oops" moment, quickly corrected by moving to a different number. (See the *High-Five Toolkit* for a diagram of the 100 square described here, as well as a list of more exercises that can be done using this grid, pp. 91–92.)
- **Use a hopscotch grid on the floor of the classroom to teach spelling:** Similarly, you can teach spelling using a hopscotch grid filled with letters (see the *High-Five Toolkit* for a diagram of this grid and other ideas for using it, pp. 165–167). When you introduce the week's spelling words, ask your students to form a circle around the Spelling Grid. Then, for each word, ask a different student to hop on each letter as the class calls them out. Linking this physical response to spelling the words keeps the students actively engaged and links the action with the correct spelling in their memories.
- **Create a physical activity to introduce or remember the core content of each lesson:** You'll find examples of this in the lesson plans at the end of the book, including students physically making acute or obtuse angles with their hands and arms (pp. 138–140), acting out historical events (pp. 140–143), or walking around pretending to be doctors treating "sick" sentences (pp. 172–178).

Make the Most of Classroom Supplies

Simply giving students an opportunity to get up out of their seats to retrieve supplies can help keep them stay alert. The change in position and the physical movement will jump start their bodies and their attention levels. If you do this creatively, you can also add humor and fun to your classroom, building a positive learning environment.

- **Let your students have fun when getting supplies:** Instead of simply saying, "Get your supplies," whenever possible, try to add creativity to these moments. For example, you might say, "Go get your whiteboard from the back of the room, but walk both ways on your tiptoes!" You'll get smiles and laughter as everyone tiptoes back to their seats, starting the lesson with high energy and positive emotions.

    You can keep changing these directions to make them even more fun. Rather than saying, "Look at me when you're ready," you might say, "Show me you're ready by balancing your whiteboard on the top of your head." Again, this is fun, but it's more than that. Balancing a whiteboard on your head actually requires concentration! Any time you ask students to balance something, you are helping them get their brains in gear for the next part of the lesson.

    You can add another dimension to this, and turn it into even more of a classroom ritual, by triggering these supply-gathering moments with music. Set it up so when your students hear a certain song, they know to get their books and dance back to their tables.

- **Students do a "paper scramble."** Green Light teachers rarely use worksheets; but when you need to distribute handouts, do it in a surprising way. You might throw the handouts high in the air, so they land all over the classroom, and your students can scramble to get one. It's a sure way to get the energy back up in your classroom.

Use Break and Celebration Moments

Finally, you can drop spontaneous opportunities for movement into your lessons to reenergize your students or to make celebrations really special.

- **Students get up and dance:** A well-placed break helps the brain to regroup. Try using designated "brain-break songs" for moments when the classroom energy fades. When you teach your rituals in the first week of school (see pp. 92–101), set it up so your students know that, if a brain-break song comes on, they should all stop whatever they are doing and simply . . . dance!
- **Students praise each other using specific movement sequences:** Try to find as many opportunities as possible for students to verbally and

physically praise each other, all the time. When setting up frequent moments of praise, to keep your students interested, you need to keep changing *how* they do this. That means getting creative and adding movement. For example, to let someone know they did a marvelous job, as a class you can set up a "hula dance of praise," where everyone does a quick hula, while saying, "Mar-ve-lous!" Or you might set up a "spirit fingers" moment: Everyone wiggles their fingers at the successful student and says, "Good job!" (Kagan & Kagan, 1998.)

Translations to Technology—Principle 4

Device	Learning Beyond Listening: Linking Action and Understanding
Computer	Computers are highly engaging, but they also run the risk of anchoring students in one place for too long. When your class is in a computer lab (with every child at their own computer), make sure you create opportunities to move between or during activities. For example: • In pairs, one student hides his eyes and the other makes a deliberate mistake on the computer. The first student is challenged to spot the mistake. Then the pair moves to the other student's computer, and the process is repeated. • When you're giving directions, ask students to "push back" from their computers, so their fingers can't touch the keyboard. When it's time to start the activity, give the command to "roll!" so students roll back to their keyboards.
iPod	Upbeat music is essential to drive movement in the classroom: Use it as a cue for different activities, as a dance track for celebrations, or as a background for learning. • Try to play content-related songs during learning activities (for example: editing could be accompanied by "ABC" by The Jackson Five, or an activity to learn the respiration system could have as its sound track "Every Breath You Take" by The Police): This will make your students smile, and it will serve as an additional memory cue.
Interactive Whiteboard	Most of your interactive whiteboard's activities are designed to get students moving, as they come up and touch the board. Choose these action-oriented activities as much as possible.
Digital Camera	Send your students on a scavenger hunt to take digital photos that support your core content. For example, if you are teaching about matter, challenge them to find a solid, liquid, and a gas to photograph.

KEY POINTS

- Physical engagement helps students grasp new material rapidly, easily committing the information to memory—often in a surprisingly short period of time.
- The most obvious benefit of engaging primary students physically is that it makes classroom management much easier.
- While teaching by talking is still a valid option for some aspects of learning, it should only be used it as a last resort.
- Physical engagement used to be a "nice to have"—now it's absolutely essential if we want to keep elementary students engaged.
- If students have to leave their seats to get supplies for the next activity, this creates a natural opportunity for movement.
- Establishing different locations in the classroom for different types of learning creates active engagement as a natural by-product of students moving from location to location.
- Movement as a part of any choral response is a simple means of making lessons more active.

5 The Learning Spiral

Building Success on Success

IMAGINATION IS THE ELIXIR OF LIFE AND THE SEED OF GREATNESS.

Breach the Dam! Success is an addictive experience. In the classroom, students should have every opportunity to encounter it, experience it, and celebrate it. As the school year passes, instead of being held back by self-doubt, they should thirst for higher and higher levels of success. It should be a universal experience for all students, of every ability level, every day. This classwide level of success fosters a mood of curiosity, interest, and excitement—a contagious atmosphere bubbling with anticipation—leading directly to high levels of engagement and, ultimately, learning.

OVERVIEW

Here's a tricky question: Did you *succeed* today? Really—think about it. Most people can't answer that question without substantial clarification. What counts as a sufficient achievement to be considered a success? Not losing your temper despite severe provocation? Finishing your grading? Changing the world? Also, what constitutes success? Total achievement? Beating your previous attempts? Or doing better than the next guy? And finally, whose measure of success are we talking about? Yours? Your mother's? Your peers'? Your students'?

As you can see, success is a more complicated idea than it may appear at first glance, in life and also at school. At one level, education's definition of success seems so simple: A student knows they have succeeded because they have done well in a test. But, let us be very careful. That definition of success is essentially *comparative*. Doing well usually means beating your fellow students. Clearly, this is an entirely appropriate interpretation in some contexts—such as a football game. As Vince Lombardi said, "If winning isn't everything, why do they keep score?" (Youth Sports Club, 2010, "Vince Lombardi's Quotes," para. 3). However, when used in a teaching environment, comparative success (where the comparison is *against* other students) can become both limiting and dangerous.

It can be limiting in the sense that this definition of success only allows a few students to succeed. This is an extremely dangerous dynamic because it sets up the clear expectation that at least some of the students must, by definition, fail. This is the bell curve result that red light teachers believe is normal: A few of my students will do very well; some will do OK; others will fail.

Let's just look at that last statement again. Does that mean our current education system is set up to *expect* failure? We take it as a simple fact of life that our school system will fail a proportion of our children. How profoundly depressing, and how damaging! Because, when students realize this dynamic, they tend to respond in three fairly distinct ways:

1. Some will dive in, determined to show they are smarter than every-one else. If they succeed, they will aggressively continue to search for more ways to prove their superiority, with the opportunity presented by every lesson and every test. They will sometimes cautiously covet—and other times publicly pronounce—their dominance over their peers.

2. Another group will approach each situation more hesitantly, uncer-tain whether it will be one in which they will succeed or not. They will be tentative in their efforts, frightened by their encounters with any lesson in which they are not immediately successful. With each subsequent failure, they become more and more withdrawn from and terrified of the learning process itself.

3. The third group will immediately form the opinion they will never be one of the smart ones; so really, why should they even try? They quickly become indifferent to all learning opportunities and fre-quently develop an attitude of resentment, which brings with it a host of behavioral problems. No amount of encouragement can get them to engage in the classroom because they believe they can't win; and, eventually, their failures will be made public, and they will face the ridicule of their peers. Better not to do anything and have nothing to be judged by.

All three of these attitudes are not only unhelpful for learning but they are also decidedly damaging. "Smart" students frequently feel guilty, and sometimes they seek to hide their successes in an attempt to fit in. Others will operate at the other end of the spectrum and use their success to taunt less-fortunate peers. Cautious students will figure out that learning is a risky proposition, indeed, and should only be engaged with in a guarded, wary manner, an attitude that severely inhibits and restricts learning. And those who believe they will never succeed develop a hardened stance towards education in general, one that is backed up and reinforced by their experiences in the classroom every day.

The result is a strongly divided classroom, creating unnecessary ten-sion and putting pressure on all your classroom activities, every day. A classroom divided against itself is a classroom on a downward spiral of disappointment. By contrast, in a Green Light classroom, there should be only *one* type of student: a curious, interested, confident, and ultimately *successful* student, one who knows that challenges lie ahead yet approaches each lesson confident that, with the correct mixture of their own efforts and the guidance of the teacher and their peers, they too will experience success.

Why is this so important? Because *learning is always emotional*, for better and for worse! On one side of the emotional spectrum lies fear—the fear of making a mistake, of embarrassment, of public *failure*. At the other end of the spectrum lies joy: the joy of discovery, of seeking answers to stimulating challenges, and of experiencing *success*. As teachers, we want to generate as many positive emotions as possible, not just because happy students are easier to teach, but because emotions have their own memory pathways (Squire, 1992, pp. 195–231). Simply put, students who constantly experience the emotional high of success throughout the learning process remember the content better!

To start our students on the road to constant success, we must carefully define the word *success* in our classrooms. We must make it clear it is not enough for students to succeed as individuals: *the whole class must succeed too.* Thus, the Green Light way of looking at success changes the game in education, at a fundamental level, by altering *what* we are comparing.

1. We are comparing an individual student's progress *only* against his individual previous abilities, knowledge, and understanding.

2. We are comparing the class's collective progress against a publicly stated standard.

These comparisons form the foundation from which all lessons and assessments are developed, and they provide the backdrop against which all actions and decisions are considered and evaluated.

The first comparison is simply a question of individual growth: Is the student moving forward? If you can find evidence that a student is moving in the right direction, then the student is doing well, and by definition, is succeeding. Thus, even seemingly small steps forward are, by definition, successes and should be celebrated both publicly and powerfully, to lock the experience of succeeding in students' hearts and minds.

The second comparison allows the class to assess their progress as a whole. This public awareness of their current rate of progress provides a sense of urgency about where they are and where they need to be. The desire to "win"—by beating other students—turns into a desire to help other students succeed, so the class can achieve collectively.

Both types of success are critical to understand and articulate, to notice and celebrate, in the classroom. They work both separately and together to foster an atmosphere of excitement, enthusiasm, and achievement. They offer all students a meaningful way of interacting with and supporting each other. When we make communal accomplishment our goal, we create a powerful dynamic of mutual self-interest that sees students helping and supporting each other rather than competing against each other.

Once the class understands what we mean by *success,* we can start putting in place the components of the Learning Spiral. When students achieve, they feel proud, pleased, and confident. They want to share their successes with friends in other classes or with their families. Succeeding brings them back the next day in search of even more achievement, and the spiral continues onward and upward. There are three essential parts of this Learning Spiral:

1. The student's *belief* in whether they can be successful;

2. The *action* they take, based on that belief; and

3. The *results* they get when they are tested.

THE LEARNING SPIRAL

Bear in mind, *each part affects the next one.* For example, if a student believes she is good in math, she will take more useful action, such as paying attention better to the lesson, asking appropriate questions, and being sure to do the assigned work in class. Subsequently, if she has paid close attention in class and done all of practice work, she will typically perform well on the test.

Of course, while the spiral can go up, it can also go down. For example, if another student believes he is not good at math, then he knows this is something he won't be successful in, so why bother? Why pay attention in class when he knows it won't do any good anyway? And if he doesn't pay attention, how can he do the work? Finally, he takes the test, and performs poorly. So how does he respond to this set of circumstances? With the simple yet incredibly destructive thought:

"See, I was right! Why bother?"

So, how do we affect students' beliefs in themselves and their abilities?

We create multiple opportunities for success and help students achieve and celebrate that success.

When this powerful cycle plays a key role in each lesson, every day, every week, students quickly begin to believe in themselves, take more useful action more often, and ultimately perform better on quizzes, texts, exams, and assessments. In this manner, the spiral moves in a positive, constructive, and affirmative direction.

IMPLEMENTATION STRATEGIES

Clearly Define *Success*

Remember the concept of *telling students everything?* This is the starting point for building attitudes about success in a Green Light classroom. Right from the beginning, make sure your students understand how you measure success and why it's important that the whole class succeeds. If we don't define a measure of success, how will they know if they are succeeding? Sometimes, it's as simple as that: By defining success, we make sure our students understand how they will achieve it.

When you get to Chapter 6 (Five-by-Five), which documents the first week of school, you'll find this idea embedded in the first day, which is deliberately set up so your students experience success quickly and get used to proudly and publicly demonstrating success, through wall charts showing individual, team, and class progress.

Success at the Lesson Level

High-Five lessons are deliberately constructed in a Learning Spiral that builds success upon success by

- Segmenting the lesson into clear, distinct steps;
- Ensuring these steps are small and easily manageable;

- Making sure all students master all steps;
- Celebrating successfully completing each step;
- Providing ultraclear instructions for any activities or interactions;
- Including a specific memory strategy; and
- Celebrating the final achievement.

Segment the Lesson Into Clear, Distinct Steps

High-Five lessons are always segmented into a distinct sequence of clear, easily manageable steps. Imagine every lesson as helping students climb from one floor of a building to the next. For most of us, getting to the next floor does not happen in a single, great, bounding leap, but as a series of small steps.

Similarly, in the classroom, as teachers we have a destination in mind: the learning objective. However, our students are unlikely to rise to the next level of understanding in a single leap. For most students, it requires a carefully modulated series of instruction, understanding, practice, and refinement. So, when designing a lesson, we need to craft steps of the appropriate size for our students' "learning legs," which will gradually lead every student to success.

Of course, some students will go up two steps at a time, making intuitive leaps of insight. This is perfectly fine, and these students should be loudly applauded for making shrewd and discerning connections. However, most students will need a clear, carefully calculated learning sequence to reach new heights of understanding.

Ensure the Steps Are Small and Easily Manageable

The *number* of steps in each lesson will vary according to a wide range of factors, including the density and complexity of the material, students' previous knowledge, and the time available. The key, however, is that there will be *many more,* and *much smaller* steps than in a traditional, red light lesson. Be sure to carefully calibrate the *level of challenge.* If something is too easy, students get bored and stop engaging with the lesson; too hard, and students get frustrated and give up. While too many steps will simply annoy everyone, if you find the right number, with the right level of challenge, and proceed up them at the right pace, you will march your students onward to success.

Make Sure All Students Master All Steps

The knowledge and understanding gained at each step provides the foundation from which they reach for the next one. It's therefore very important that all students master each step before the class moves on to the next step. Before you dismiss this as too hard, remember that these steps are frequently smaller chunks of learning than in traditional education. You'll be surprised how easy this is to accomplish, and you will be delighted with the progress you'll see from students who previously struggled to grasp core concepts.

Celebrate Each Successful Step

Of course, the successful completion of *each rung* is a cause for celebration! The idea of having *multiple* moments of celebration may surprise some teachers, as it goes against the traditional belief that celebration or acknowledgment is only to be done at the completion of an entire lesson, if at all. However, joyful celebration adds a critical ingredient: uplifting, positive emotions, which lead to the desire for more of the same, propelling the lesson forward. Acknowledgment, recognition, celebration, and festivity are the nails that hold the treads of the staircase together and keep students confident they will ultimately reach the top.

Multiple moments of high spirits also play a small, but crucial, role in the overall success of your lesson. They provide a clear signal that a segment of the lesson is complete. This simultaneously signals the start of a *new* segment. Students tend to naturally perk up and pay close attention at the start of anything new; so once again, they're primed and ready to learn. Because it is taught in segments, *a single High-Five lesson will have many beginnings and endings.*

Student Celebration Strategies

Here are some specific ways your students can celebrate their successes. The key is to move away from the teacher saying, "Well done," and instead allow students to celebrate with each other (Jensen, 2006, p. 262).

- Students give each other high fives, or high tens.
- Students make up a creative high fives—such as behind-the-back fives or under-the-legs threes.
- Celebrate as a class, all together saying something such as, "We rock!"
- Invent a class clap: a specific sequence or pattern.
- Invent a special celebration noise or sound.
- Create a funny dance or a dramatic pose that everyone does to celebrate class success.

Here are some examples of special cheers:

- Students wave their arms in a hula dance and say, "Mar-ve-lous!"
- Students shake hands with two or three others, saying, "Handy idea!"
- Students make a rocket sound and say, "Out of this world!"
- Students push their hands toward the ceiling, saying, "Go us! Go us! Go Us!"
- Students put a finger on top of their heads, make a sizzling sound, and say, "My brain is hot, hot, hot!"

Include a Specific Memory Strategy

One critical aspect of a High-Five lesson is including a step *specifically dedicated to a memory strategy.* While this can appear at any point—when first introducing the topic, during the lesson, or in summarizing the lesson—it *must* be included somewhere.

For example, you might begin a lesson by telling a story (Caine & Caine, 1994, p. 92). At first, your students may see no relevance to the story; but as the lesson unfolds, they discover all the key information in the lesson was concealed within the story, and they excitedly share with each other where different parts of the lesson are hidden in the story. Later, to remember the key ideas, they only have to remember the story, and all the key ideas from the lesson will tumble out of their head.

Or, at the end of a lesson, your might list the key trigger words or ideas and for students to memorize using the peg system—see the *High-Five Toolkit*—or any other memory strategy[1]. Students may do this individually, in pairs, or in teams.

Note: this step is done *in class,* during class time, under your guidance, direction, and supervision. Never set memorization as homework. Deliberately using a memory strategy not only reinforces the information in your lesson but also strengthens your students' confidence in their abilities. Success with any memory strategy evokes a powerful feeling of accomplishment, making your students anticipate the next lesson with excitement—not dread.

This leads to one final point. While memory strategies are intrinsic to the success of any lesson, sometimes within a unit students might go through several related lessons. In this situation, the memory strategy might not be used until all the related lessons have been taught. Then, you might create a single memory strategy that brings them all together.

Give Ultraclear Instructions

If a step includes any type of interaction or activity, the success of that step is often dependent on how well it is structured. This means our instructions must be clean, precise, allowing no room for misunderstanding and confusion. This, often overlooked, aspect of teaching is often the pivotal point around which an activity flourishes or fails[2].

Success at the Daily Level

At the end of each day, check in with your students. Bring them together for an opportunity to figuratively—or perhaps even literally—high five each other. To do this, allow 5 to 10 minutes for students to voice some positive comments about their classmates.

During this time, a student might say, "I want to give Bobby a high five because he helped me with my math." Or, a student might say, "My team really worked well together today—we helped each other the whole time!" After each student response, make sure the class thanks him or her for sharing. This opportunity to share positive thoughts with the entire class, at the end of each day, means your students leave on an optimistic, upbeat note. Walking out of the room in this way significantly affects how they walk in the next day—giving them a great attitude from which to approach the next chunk of learning.

Success at the Unit Level

While the Learning Spiral is foundational to the design of any lesson, it is also central to the structure and flow of a unit. To build the idea of the Learning Spiral into a unit of study, a High-Five teacher will typically follow this general sequence:

Day One

- Teacher introduces the concept, perhaps with a story, discussion, conversation, or group activity.
- Students talk about it, live it, act it out.

Day Two

- Teacher makes the concept real and concrete through further explanation, clarification, or elaboration as needed.

- Students practice the concept. This is *seldom done individually*, especially in the early stages of learning; usually it is done in pairs, trios, or teams.

Day Three

- Students demonstrate their understanding of the concept in one of many ways, perhaps by retelling it, drawing it, modeling it, or doing a demonstration that shows it in action.

Day Four

- Students practice or revisit their memory strategy if it was introduced earlier.

Day Five

- Students walk in on test day confident!

Success Here, There, and Everywhere

While the ideas shown so far are all designed and developed to build success upon success, here are some additional ways we can continue to keep positive energy alive in the classroom.

- **No red pens!** When grading papers, *never use a red pen*. As adults, many of us relate the color red to "Danger!" or "Warning" or simply to a stop sign. Yet even at a very young age, the color red, when used in the classroom, has a negative association for many students. It can easily turn potentially useful feedback—or any type of constructive criticism—into something they instinctively rebel against. Use any bright color: blue, purple, or green! It's no accident that Green Light teachers often use green pens: If students associate it to anything, it's usually something positive, or happy. Green in a traffic light means *"Go!"*
- **Personal chats:** If a student happens to have a lapse in success, and earns a low grade, always be certain to speak to them *personally*, before they see the grade. Let them know you understand this is not their normal pattern, and it happens to everyone occasionally. Then, if possible, give that student additional opportunities to retest the same information until they achieve success.

- **How many are *correct*?** When grading papers, quizzes, or tests, never put the number *wrong* at the top of the page! This points students' focus in an entirely inappropriate direction. Instead, always total up the *correct* answers, and put that number at the top of the page. This shows how their efforts have paid off so far and hopefully points them in the right direction.
- **Chart their success:** When students receive graded papers, be sure to give them an opportunity to graph their success, as shown in Figure 6.5 on page 112. Have them make an individual graph to show their growth over time. This way, if they happen to receive one lower grade, they can see for themselves that it truly was a one-time event, and they can remind themselves they really are capable of doing better next time.

At the heart of this principle lies a clear distinction: Red light teachers believe that for the educational system to succeed, some students must ultimately fail. On the other hand, Green Light teachers view the process of learning from an entirely different perspective. They believe

All students can succeed, if they are shown how.

Our focus, then, is to find ways of teaching that allow students to succeed. And when they succeed, we must immediately celebrate with them, help them see the power of their achievements, and by doing so, propel the Learning Spiral ever onwards and upwards.

Case Study

After school, a Green Light teacher was preparing for the next day's class. She had written some information for the students on the chalkboard. A red light teacher stopped by to chat and, looking at the chalkboard, said, "Hey, this word is misspelled!" But the Green Light Teacher smiled and said, "You're in my class now, and that means you have to follow our rules!" "What rules?" the red light teacher asked. "Well," said the Green Light teacher, "before you're allowed to tell me how many words I misspelled, *first you have to tell me how many words I spelled correctly!* Only then can you tell me about any "creative spelling choices" I've made!" The red light teacher didn't understand and left puzzled. The Green Light teacher and her class exchanged secret smiles . . .

Translations to Technology—Principle 5

Device	The Learning Spiral: Building success on success
Computer	On the class Web site, post a Cheers section where the class test graph is displayed as well as other celebrations.
iPod	Use songs as memory strategies. • Create new words to well-known tunes to help your students remember core content, or get your students to write their own "learning lyrics." • You can download karaoke (music without lyrics) versions of most well-known songs. Prepare for a test by singing along with your new lyrics. Have a number of celebration songs high on your play list, so they are always easy to find.
Interactive Whiteboard	Show progress of a particular lesson on the interactive whiteboard, marking off the steps as the class has completed them.
Digital Camera	Celebrate the successful completion of each small step with a "photo opportunity." This will both clearly show students that even partial success is worthy of celebration and motivate them to complete each step more quickly—to earn their moment of glory. Take digital photos of students and their awards. Print them out for inclusion in students' "brag books" or for their profile on the class Web site.

KEY POINTS

- Success is a *naturally addictive experience,* driving students to ever higher levels of engagement as they seek to repeat their previous achievement.
- Success should be a universal experience for all students, of every ability level, every day, in every classroom.
- Success should be competitive only as it applies to a student's own performance record, never as it applies to comparing one student against another.
- It is not enough for individual students to succeed: They must support the whole class succeeding too.
- For students to succeed, the *level of challenge* must be appropriate.
- More students will succeed if teachers segment lessons into clear, distinct steps and ensure these steps are small and easily manageable.
- *All* students can remember content, if they are given a specific memory strategy.
- Every success, no matter how small, should be celebrated.

6 Five-by-Five

Setting the Stage for Student Success

OVERVIEW

This section provides step-by-step instructions for setting up a Green Light classroom in the first week of school, including preparing the physical environment before the students arrive and embedding the classroom rituals and routines that will underpin this new way of teaching. If you've been reading the High-Five Principles and thinking, "This is all very well, but it wouldn't work in *my* classroom . . ." you're probably right. The Principles probably wouldn't work in your classroom *with its current setup rituals, and approaches.* Depending on how you currently teach, you'll need to make certain adjustments to make sure the dynamics in your classroom support the High-Five Principles. In other words, you have to prepare your students for a whole new approach to learning. The suggestions in this section may be radically different from the usual way you approach the first week of school (in fact, they should be). If you're going to get substantially better learning outcomes, you will probably need to change quite a number of things in your classroom. Don't worry if the following ideas seem strange or even counterintuitive: They have all been tested in real classrooms with phenomenal results.

As you start to look through this section, keep in mind one important thing: It has been specifically designed for the start of a new school year. However, almost everything in this section will be just as effective at the beginning of a semester, and many of the ideas can be introduced at any time. All it takes is a little bit of adaptation and adjustment.

Preparations Before the First Day of School

Because you're going to be running your classroom differently, you need to set it up and resource it differently too.

Physically Creating a Fluid Classroom

Form follows function. A Green Light classroom is interactive, communal, and constantly in motion—with learning locations and modalities changing frequently. If your classroom has rows of desks and assigned seating, your first task is to move your furniture! Figure 6.1 shows the sort of layout you should aim for.

Figure 6.1 Classroom Setup

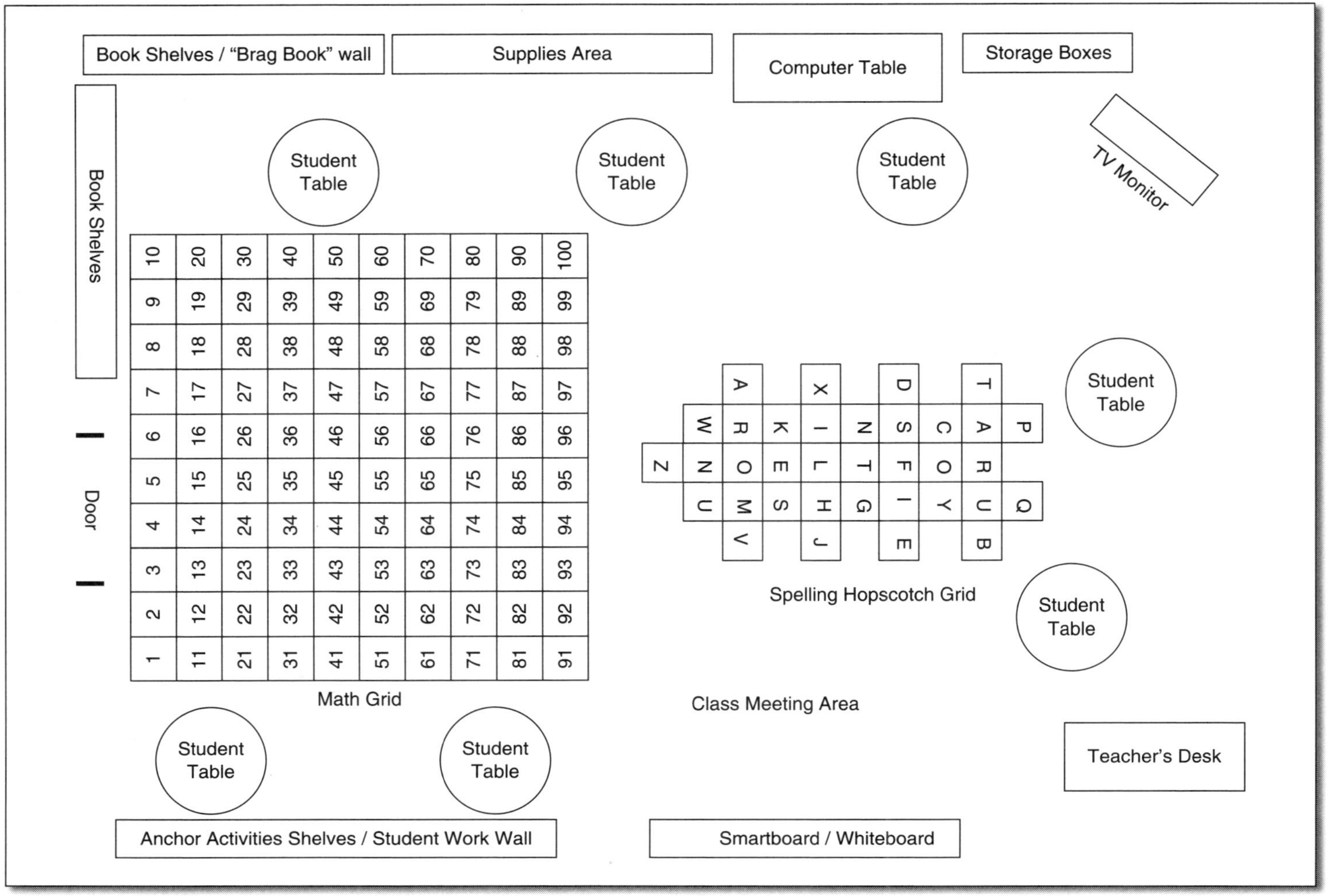

Book Shelves / "Brag Book" wall

Supplies Area

Computer Table

Storage Boxes

TV Monitor

Student Table

Student Table

Student Table

Student Table

Student Table

Student Table

Teacher's Desk

Smartboard / Whiteboard

Class Meeting Area

Spelling Hopscotch Grid

		P		Q	
T	A	R	U	B	
	C	O	Y		
D	S	F	I	E	
	N	T	G		
X	I	L	H	J	
	K	E	S		
A	R	O	M	V	
	W	N	U		
	Z				

Math Grid

1	2	3	4	5	6	7	8	9	10
11	12	13	14	15	16	17	18	19	20
21	22	23	24	25	26	27	28	29	30
31	32	33	34	35	36	37	38	39	40
41	42	43	44	45	46	47	48	49	50
51	52	53	54	55	56	57	58	59	60
61	62	63	64	65	66	67	68	69	70
71	72	73	74	75	76	77	78	79	80
81	82	83	84	85	86	87	88	89	90
91	92	93	94	95	96	97	98	99	100

Anchor Activities Shelves / Student Work Wall

Book Shelves

Door

Ten key features of this layout deserve special mention.

1. Try to get round tables instead of individual desks. If this is not possible, turn the desks so that the cubby part is *not accessible*. Make "cooperative pods" of desks that serve as a larger table. This does two things: It adds space by getting desks closer to each other, and it takes away the "It's *my* desk!" attitude. To have a successfully fluid environment, students need to move happily from place to place. They will only do this if they don't "own" one particular spot in the room.

2. Your students will need plenty of space to move. However you design your room, make sure you maximize the amount of space you have for movement.

3. Create an "anchor activities" shelf. This is an area specially set aside with backup sheets for regular activities. This prevents students from interrupting the flow of a lesson by saying, "I don't have that paper!" Instead, they know there are always extra forms available, and they are free to immediately go get one, on their own (Fisher & Frey, 2008, pp. 32–37). Your anchor activities shelf might include things such as:

   • Book project report sheets
   • Self-edit forms
   • Peer edit forms
   • Weekly self-examination forms
   • Blank notebook paper
   • Spelling sheets
   • Writing sheets
   • Social studies sheets
   • Doodle-Predict sheets (see the High-Five Toolkit)
   • Prewrite graphic organizer forms

4. The Spelling Grid and Math 100-Square Grid are made of masking tape, and they stay on the classroom floor for the entire year. Their creation and use are discussed in depth in the High-Five Toolkit (pp. 165–171).

5. Don't put nametags on tables. As you'll soon discover, you're going to let students sit wherever they feel comfortable on the first day of school. Sitting by people you know brings the affective filter down and the potential for learning up. Don't worry about students getting distracted when sitting with their friends, seating arrangements will change frequently anyway.

6. Create a "meeting area." Keep one section of the classroom free of any furniture, so your students can sit on the floor and direct their

attention to you. If you don't have room to create this permanent space, designate an area where the class can meet with a minimum amount of furniture moving required. For example, choose a corner of the classroom where, if desks are pushed back, there is sufficient room for all students to gather together, some seated on the floor and others perched on the edges of the desks.

7. Share supplies. A true Green Light classroom is a communal classroom: All supplies are shared, with students returning them daily. This eliminates the "I don't have a pencil" syndrome. It also teaches students to share supplies amicably. So, create a supply storage cupboard or shelf in a central area that can be easily accessed by your students.

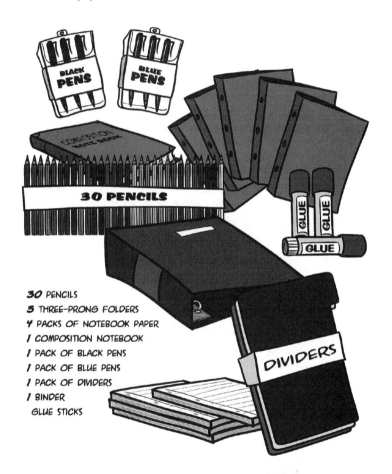

8. Send out notes for parents. If possible, send out your supply list before school starts. This note should inform parents that all supplies will be for general (not individual) use in the classroom. They should not be labeled with the student's names and should be basic, generic supplies (no flashy, expensive pens or pencils). The

note should also ask parents to send in photographs of a student's families and friends to share with the class.

9. Store your textbooks. You're only going to use textbooks occasionally as a reference resource—never for students to "read individually and answer questions at the end of the chapter." So, you'll want to designate an area of the classroom to keep all your textbooks. One easy option is to stack the books in bins on the floor, or on a bookshelf in groups of four or five (depending upon how large your cooperative teams are). One student from each team will be the designated supplier in charge of grabbing the books when needed.

10. Make room for year-long projects. Put up your usual visuals and posters, but leave at least two areas or bulletin boards open. Keep one for charting the class's progress. Keep another for your students to express their own interests, share family photos, or proudly display certificates (Swartz, 2008, p. 26–31).

DAY 1: STARTING WITH A BANG!

How Your Students Are Feeling

Many students start the year with negative emotions. They may be disappointed that the first day of school signals the end of their summer of freedom. They may be worried because their best friend is in another class or nervous about what will be expected of them in this new, more difficult grade. Many will be unsure of what their new teacher will ask of them. Perhaps most importantly, many of them may have a strong expectation that today will be *boring*.

Your Goal

Demonstrate that this classroom is *different*, and give your students a reason to look forward to coming to school tomorrow.

Why?

This is by far the most important day of the entire school year for one reason: From the very first minute, students form a powerfully persistent perception of you and the classroom. Whatever happens on this day will shape their attitude for the rest of the year. If you present your students with the same old "getting to know you" or "classroom rules" activities they have done many times before, you are playing to their expectation that this year will be more of the same.

However, if you do something different and show them something they have never seen before, you will seize their attention, raise the startling idea that learning can actually be fun, and get them excited about the possibilities of the new year.

How?

In a Green Light classroom, we explode the myth of "school is boring," the instant students walk through the door, by creating a positive, upbeat, and highly *different* experience to what they're expecting.

Suggested Schedule for Day One

8:00–8:30: Welcome

Greet students as they enter the room

Play the song, "I Can See Clearly Now" by Jimmy Cliff.

Allow students to sit anywhere they want to.

Activity: Students individually draw a picture of everything they *wish* they did on their summer vacation.

8:30–9:00: Physical Education (P.E.)

Begin by introducing them to the idea of how to line up to the song "Pretty Woman" by Roy Orbison.

9:00–9:30: Introductions

Students share their pictures with each other in pairs, explaining what they drew and why they included it.

Introduce yourself. Show personal family pictures.

Ask students to share the photos they brought in.

Begin a "Friends and Family" wall where students post their photos.

9:30–10:00: Memory Pegs

Demonstration and introduction—seeing the pegs in action.

10:00–10:30: Practice—learning the pegs.

10:30–11:00: Application—using the pegs to remember content.

11:00–11:30: Teambuilding

Each team of 4 or 5 creates team artwork on large puzzle pieces, with each student's name on one of the pieces. This demonstrates how—as a team—they all "fit together."

(Continued)

(Continued)

11:30–12:00: Class Meeting

Topic: Students share what they did over the summer. As they do this, they are asked to model correct classroom behavior.

12:00–1:00: Lunch

1:00–1:30: Spelling Grid Introduction

1:30–2:00: 100-Square Grid for Math Introduction

2:00–2:30: Journal Reflection

Students write in about their day: What they expected, what they learned, and what they are looking forward to tomorrow.

2:30–2:35: Reset

Students clean up the room, then they are invited to *hop* out the door to the song "Hit the Road Jack" by Ray Charles.

Optional Homework: Teach their parents the Memory Pegs!

Welcome

Greet your students with music (Peretz & Zatorre, 2005, pp. 89–114). Choose catchy, upbeat tunes such as "Pretty Woman," "Round The Clock," "Brown-Eyed Girl," "At the Hop," or "Rockin' Robin."

Other than making your classroom different, lively music has many additional benefits. It sets a positive emotional tone and provides a "sound cover" under which students can comfortably chat to each other before you start the lesson. It also gives you a mechanism for getting attention. When you want to start, instead of raising your voice, you can simply raise the volume of the music. When the music gets so loud the students can no longer hear each other, they will turn to look at you. At that moment, cut the music dead, and speak into the stunned silence: "Good morning! Welcome to your new classroom!"

As your students arrive, make a point of telling students they can sit wherever they like. This is an important message on the first day. It says to your students, "This is *your* classroom—*you* get to choose." These simple welcoming techniques will change your students' emotional state. Sitting with their friends, listening to fun music, chatting away, they are happy and comfortable; they are also curious: This classroom is different! These students are ripe for learning.

Memory Pegs

Early in the first day, you come to one of the most important lessons you will ever teach. Your goal is to teach your students something they didn't think they could do—and make it fun. This will deliver three vital messages:

1. I can succeed in this classroom.

2. I can learn from this teacher.

3. Learning isn't boring.

How do you do this? You teach them how to memorize things—very rapidly—using the following Memory Pegs.

The Peg	The Action
1. Sun	Make a circle with your hands.
2. Eyes	Bring two fingers to your eyes.
3. Triangle	Draw a triangle in the air with your fingers.
4. Stove	Touch all four burners on a stove.
5. Fingers	Hold up the five fingers of one hand.
6. Sticks	Pick up sticks from the ground.
7. 7 Up	Take a big drink from a can of 7-Up.
8. Octopus	Put your arms out like an octopus.
9. Line	Draw a line in the air in front of you.
10. Hen	Flap your arms like a chicken's wings.
11. Fence	Put two fingers in the air, and make a series of fence posts.
12. Eggs	Crack an imaginary egg.
13. Black Cat	Pet the cat.
14. Heart	Make a heart in the air in front of you with your fingers.
15. Fame	Spread your arms wide, and say, "Fame!"
16. Driving	Drive an imaginary car.
17. Magazine	Turn the pages of an imaginary magazine.
18. Vote	Make a check mark in the air.
19. TV	Click the imaginary remote at the imaginary TV.
20. 20–20 Vision	Make circles with your hands around your eyes.

Here's how you use them. First, ask students to name 20 random household items to put on the board. Write these up as they call them out. Then, you use the pegs to "memorize" these 20 things in 30 seconds! (How to do this is explained in depth in the High-Five Toolkit.) Next, you teach your students how to memorize these 20 things, just like you did! Imagine the scene:

To your students' amazement, you instantly memorize a list of 20 items. You then tell them, "Within 45 minutes, you'll be able to do the same thing!" They stare at you in disbelief, but in that short time, accompanied by music and laughter, you teach your students the first 20 memory pegs and how to use them. Sure enough, at the end of the lesson, every student has successfully memorized the list. They are triumphant: they have experienced success as a *direct result* of your teaching. The sheer power of this moment can drive the rest of your school year. From this one activity, your students learn they can trust you. Once they trust you, the sky is the limit.

By teaching students memory pegs on the first day, you also empower them with vital learning tools they will use throughout the school year. In a Green Light classroom, we always teach students *how* to remember.

Build Your Teams

As most of the activities for the week hinge on students working in teams, it's a good idea to both create teams and allocate to each student a team job on the very first day of school. Give each team their own wall area, where they can put up their artwork and record team successes.

- This *first week,* let *them* choose their own team. This reinforces the idea of student ownership, giving students choices in the classroom.
- The *second week,* make sure you choose the teams, based on what you've observed about their personalities, and mixing and matching learning levels appropriately.
- Finally, change teams *every month.* This gives students the opportunity to work with different students. It also allows them to sit in different parts of the room, which helps them feel the entire classroom is theirs and stops them becoming overly protective of their "turf."

Sorting Ability Levels in Teams

As much as possible, try to have mixed ability levels in the teams you choose, so students have the opportunity to help each other and to learn from their peers.

However, *be careful of placing the highest-performing students in groups with lowest-performing students.* While occasionally this strategy will be effective, many times the gap in understanding and ability levels is simply too wide for students to bridge easily. Low-performing students may simply see the gap between where they are and where the high-performing students are as too big to realistically cross. Equally important, high-performers often can't see why other students don't get it.

Instead, try to place students together in teams with students of somewhat *similar skill levels.* In this way, the space between skill levels is not as great, and thus students are often more able to help each other—and less likely to get frustrated. The interactions between students of somewhat similar skill levels often leads to exciting, dynamic, and useful classroom conversations.

Because it will take you a while to figure out individual abilities, here's a method for quickly sorting students into somewhat *similar* skill levels. Label the four corners of the room (either with a written sign or just verbally) as follows:

Corner 1: A narrow, rough, dirt road

Corner 2: A nicely paved street

Corner 3: A highway

Corner 4: The yellow brick road

To use this metaphor, tell your students you'd like to ask about how they view themselves in terms of their understanding of math skills. You ask them if they are

- On the "dirt road" of learning, where their understanding still has a long way to go, and sometimes it takes them quite a bit of practice to really feel confident about a concept;
- On a "paved street" of learning, where they feel sure they'll understand it eventually, but it might take a while;
- On the "highway" of learning, where once they are taught something, they pick it up really fast; or
- On the "yellow brick road" of learning, where they feel really great about their understanding, and would almost call themselves a math wiz.

Ask students to walk to the area they think best describes their current ability level. Based on your observations, you could then consider organizing teams of "road" learners and "street" learners, and other teams of "highway" learners and "yellow brick road" learners. This will reduce the differences in understanding between team members, producing better levels of student coaching.

Of course, this road metaphor is just one way you could use the idea of the four corners of the room; any other four-part, sequential metaphor would fit. For example, boats: from a raft in corner one, up to a cruise ship in corner four. Or, felines: from a kitten in corner one, up to a lion in corner four.

Team Names

Once the teams are formed, let each group choose a team name. The first team-building exercise could then be to create a team logo or a team handshake.

Team Jobs

Now it's time to assign team jobs. On day three, you'll expand the idea of team jobs. However, for this first day, keep it very straight forward, so students can become acclimated to the idea of everyone having a specific role to play within the group. The four basic team job titles could be:

- Super Supplier—responsible for getting any supplies needed for team activities.
- Perfect Praiser—responsible for ensuring appropriate levels of praise and acknowledgment are being maintained and delivered promptly.
- Neat Freak—responsible for keeping the team area clean and tidy at all times.
- Team Manager—responsible for making sure all work is completed on time and everyone is contributing equally to every activity.

Team Points

The second team activity should help them create a place where they can earn points. For example, students could create a team puzzle made of an interlocking piece for each team member. Each team member's piece of the puzzle would include her name as well as any decorations she might want to add. Points would then be earned for things such as:

- Cooperating with each other;
- Praising each other;
- Taking "learning positions" rapidly;
- Completing transitions smoothly and quickly; and
- Returning things on time.

Whenever a team earns a point for any particular behavior, record it at the bottom of their team puzzle chart, so students can keep close track of how many points their team has earned. Note: In a Green Light classroom, *points are never taken away.* Adding points is moving forward in a positive direction—a focal point of almost every choice and decision made in a Green Light classroom. Removing points is a negative response to a situation—the *opposite* of what we are trying to achieve!

And, what's in it for the team with the most points? While it could certainly be a wide array of things, here's a creative option: After two weeks, perhaps the team with the most points gets to eat lunch with the teacher! This avoids having the reward be something physical, and yet is something very real—and exciting—to elementary students.

Class Meeting

Your first class meeting is another important landmark. Tell your students that, every week, you will set aside a time for students to voluntarily share what is going on in their lives with the group for about 15 minutes. This will soon become the most important 15 minutes of your week. The meetings serve three main purposes, giving you an opportunity to

1. Gain information about the students' lives;

2. Model correct behavior; and

3. Create a safe environment in which students can share.

You can learn so much about your students by simply asking about their weekend (Wolk, 2008, pp. 8–14). You gain insight and perspective. Most important, students see that you care about them individually.

When each student shares, make a point to respond to his story with specific comments or a question. This models good listening skills for the rest of the students. Next, always thank the student for sharing. Again, the modeling is critical to set the proper tone of the class. No student should be coerced into sharing. It should always be a natural choice. Even if certain students never share, they reap the benefits of seeing what real, positive communication looks like. In a world of texting and e-mail, most students today lack basic social graces when interacting with each other simply because they rarely have the chance to see or experience it.

Once your students settle in, you only hold a class meeting once a week. However, for the first week, you need a class meeting *every day* to reinforce the routine and model listening skills.

Spelling Grid Introduction

Your students will have been wondering why there is a hopscotch grid with letters on the floor of your classroom, so this is an exciting moment for them.

Explain that, this year, students will learn their spelling words by hopping out the letters! Teach them how to use the grid shown in Figure 6.2 and run through an example lesson, as described in detail in the High-Five Toolkit (pp. 164–167).

Figure 6.2 Spelling Grid

Figure 6.3 Math Grid

1	2	3	4	5	6	7	8	9	10
11	12	13	14	15	16	17	18	19	20
21	22	23	24	25	26	27	28	29	30
31	32	33	34	35	36	37	38	39	40
41	42	43	44	45	46	47	48	49	50
51	52	53	54	55	56	57	58	59	60
61	62	63	64	65	66	67	68	69	70
71	72	73	74	75	76	77	78	79	80
81	82	83	84	85	86	87	88	89	90
91	92	93	94	95	96	97	98	99	100

Introduce Students to the Math 100-Square Grid

Next, move to the math grid in Figure 6.3 (also discussed in Principle 4 on pages 168–171), where you can explain that math will also be different this year because students will be jumping their math problems!

Show your students how this will work. For example, all students might be asked to stand on any number. Then, they are asked to, "Add 7, and stand on the answer," or "Subtract 9, and stand on the answer." See the High-Five Toolkit for a more detailed discussion of how to use the 100-Square Grid.

DAY 2: ESTABLISHING ROUTINES AND RITUALS

How Your Students Are Feeling

If the first day went well, then today you have a huge advantage—your students trust you. By now, you have established that when you make a promise to them, you will follow through. Yesterday, your students experienced the high of achievement (with the Memory Pegs, Spelling Grid, and Math Grid); they were given choices (where to sit); they were listened to (class meetings); and they had fun and celebrated. They should be excited—or at the very least open minded and curious—about what you have in store for them today.

Your Goal

Show your students exactly how you want them to behave; set up nonvocal cues for regular classroom routines and rituals, such as lining up, or physical and vocal celebrations, and establish classroom communication protocols.

Why?

Taking the time in the first few days to perfect the behavior and *exact* actions you desire from the students will save hours—if not days or even weeks—of time later. If you establish the tone of good behavior at the start of the year, you save the headache of constantly reminding students to behave later. Clear, consistent cues provide certainty about what you expect of students at all times and help develop and maintain the sense of trust needed to maximize effective learning in a Green Light classroom. You will need to practice the cues over the first week and beyond. But, the more your students practice and get accustomed to the proper way to do things, the more your classroom will become smooth running, efficient, and well mannered.

How?

Suggested Schedule for Day Two

8:00–8:30: **Welcome**

Give each student a high five as he or she walks into the room.

Again, play the song "I Can See Clearly Now."

Activity: Each student draws a self-portrait.

8:30–9:00: **P.E.** As demonstrated in day one, students line up to "Pretty Woman."

9:00–9:30: **Memory Pegs Practice**

Practice as a whole class, then in pairs, and then in teams.

Celebrate with students giving each other high fives.

(Continued)

(Continued)

9:30–10:00: **Library Class**

Each student checks out a book appropriate to their reading level. (Note: If they always have a book to read when they complete activities, they will be less idle, more productive, and behavior-management issues are less likely to arise.)

10:00–10:30: **Music Cues Introduction**—practice each cue.

10:30–11:00: **Silent Cues Introduction**—practice each cue.

11:00–11:30: **Student Cues Introduction**—practice each cue.

11:30–12:00: **Class Meeting**

Students share what their parents said about the pegs. (Remind them to model correct class-meeting behavior.)

12:00–1:00: **Lunch**

1:00–1:30: **Learning Games**—100-Square and Spelling Grids

1:30–2:00: **How Am I Smart?**

Teach the ways people are smart: music, people, picture, body, word, self, nature, number.

Students complete diagnostic questionnaire titled "In Which Ways Are You Smart?" (see the High-Five Toolkit, p. 179).

Students cut out their self-portrait and paste it to a big piece of construction paper. They title the paper: "I am smart in these ways!" Then they list the ways in which they are smart.

2:00–2:30: **Journal Reflection**

Students write about their day.

2:30–2:35: **Reset**

Students clean up the room then *hop* out the door to "Hit the Road Jack."

Always start the day with some upbeat music. Today, start with the same song as yesterday. Your students will recognize it and go back to the relaxed state of the day before. Then, begin a day of team-building activities and plenty of chances to *learn and practice their cues*.

Self-Portrait

The goal here is for students to produce something creative that shows something about themselves (it's not a test of drawing ability). These could be simple line drawings of a basic face shape on construction paper with their names underneath and the images filled in with words they believe describe themselves, such as *fun, honest, trustworthy,* and so on. Or, they could work with a partner to trace their profile from their shadow on the wall and then fill their profile with a collage of images cut from magazines. These are just a few possibilities. The key is for students to understand that who they are and what they like are important in this classroom.

Explaining the Cues to Students

Use the following three-step sequence to help your students understand the idea of cues and why they are being used in the classroom:

1. If possible, model the cues even before they are ever mentioned.

2. Simply point out what has been happening.

3. Discuss with students why using a cue might be helpful to everyone.

For example, to establish a music cue for forming a line at the door:

1. On day one, every time you ask students to form a line, make sure your line-up cue song is playing quite loudly. Be sure to repeat this several times during the day.

2. Next, at the start of day two, you might say, "Did you notice every time you lined up at the door a certain song was playing? What song was it?" Once they identify the song, you say, "Let's use that as our signal to line up! Every time that song comes on, it'll mean it's time to form a line at the door!"

3. Finally, lead a class meeting and discuss *why* it might be helpful to use cues. Instead of telling students why you are doing this, ask them! Their responses will usually include ideas such as, "It helps you save your voice!" and, "It helps *all* of us know what to do, right away!" and, "It helps us work together as a group." As a result of this conversation, students will see the value of cues. Understanding why cues are both useful and necessary will help them accept the idea more readily and thus respond to the cues more rapidly.

Music Cues

Choose four upbeat songs that you enjoy (something you can listen to everyday for the entire school year). You will need

- One song for lining up (e.g., "Pretty Woman" by Roy Orbison);
- One song for transition periods, (e.g., "Three Little Birds" by Bob Marley);
- One for celebrations (e.g., "Boogie Shoes" by KC & The Sunshine band); and
- One for cleaning up at the end of the day (e.g., "At The Hop" by Danny & The Juniors).

When practicing, if any student does not respond to the cue, pause and make the necessary adjustment. Do not go on to something else until everyone understands the cue and is responding to it properly. Fixing problems now means fixing less later!

Please note: *You do not need to play these songs in their entirety;* only play them until your desired actions are accomplished. Sometimes, you may only play the celebration song for 30 seconds. These songs are cues, triggers to elicit a desired reaction. You may only need the trigger playing for 30 or 45 seconds.

Lining Up

Introduce your students to the first few seconds of your line-up song, tell them *exactly* where and how you want them to line, and then give them lots of opportunities to practice. Now is the time to remind them that they must line up in an orderly manner. Take the time to iron out the kinks in behavior now, right here at the beginning, *before* you try to use the cues for real. Students need to practice doing the action in the correct way several times to establish a routine. Later, you might consider having certain teams line up first on certain days. For now, though, be sure to establish the order early on, and keep to the order of your routine.

Transitions

Introduce your transition song *in context first* without your students knowing it is the cue song. When you finish an activity on the first and second days of school, as you transition to another activity, play the song. When you have done this a few times, ask the students if they recognized hearing a certain song at certain times. When they realize what the song means, then you can introduce the specific actions you need to see when the song is played.

For example, the action might be to put up the materials for the current activity and to give you an "I'm ready" sign indicating they are ready for the next activity. As novelty and creativity are a huge part of a Green Light classroom, here are some suggestions for I'm ready signs:

- Students put on some funny-shaped sunglasses
- Students sit in a "ready position," knees toward you
- Students put their hands on their heads
- Students interlock their fingers
- Students give you a big smile

Choose an action you believe the students will enjoy doing throughout the year. Once you have the transition cue modeled, practice it several times, and work out the behavior issues now. Once again, it is critical to set very clear and very specific expectations for student behavior in a Green Light classroom.

Celebrations

Choose an appropriate celebration song, such as:

"Celebration" by Kool and the Gang

"That's the Way I Like It" by Kool and the Gang

"New Attitude" by Patti La Belle

"Funkytown" by Lipps, Inc.

"Get Up and Boogie" by Silver Convention

"You Should Be Dancing" by The Bee Gees

"Rock the Boat" by The Hues Corporation

"Good Times" by Chic

Remember, these are just suggestions. Use whatever works for you and your students! Try to choose one that makes people want to get up and dance.

Again, first use the celebration song in context without explanation. When the students master something as a class or end a lesson successfully, play the celebration song. Encourage the students to get up and dance if they want to—this might be a good time to model appropriate dancing! Use this song *as many times as possible* in the first two days.

When you explain that the meaning of this song is a cue to celebrate, talk about how this year the whole class is going to be very successful, and how it's important to celebrate success. Ask your students to name some of the times they've been successful already so far this week. Get them talking about the things they're good at. The message is that "We can all succeed, and we will all celebrate everyone's success."

Cleaning Up

Choose a clean-up song that is at least two to three minutes long. The first time you introduce it, be sure to play this song in its entirety, daily. To introduce this song as a cue, first model the actions you want to see when the song comes on, showing how they are to return all supplies to their proper places and organize their group table. Then, ask teams to practice the actions several times. Have fun by first allowing them one minute to mess up their table, placing everything in disarray. Then, play the song, and let them put everything away. The goal is for them to be done and ready to do something else by the end of the song. Repeat this several times until the start of the song truly triggers this behavior in all students.

Music cues, introduced and used appropriately, can be a very powerful means of running a classroom. Once a song is linked to physical memory with an action, the desired reaction is powerfully programmed. The same can be done with silent—visual—cues.

Silent Cues

The process for establishing silent cues is slightly different. First, explain and demonstrate each one, and give specific examples of the desired reaction. Then, get your students to practice. This will require some patience on your part, but it will be worth it in saving your voice throughout the year as well as for the clarity in classroom communication it develops. You can establish any number of silent cues, but you'll need at least three basic ones in a Green Light classroom: class meeting, quiet, and attention (stop what you are doing). Remember, when setting each cue: explain, model, practice.

Class-Meeting Cue

Every week starts with a class meeting, and most lessons will start with the students sitting in the class meeting area, hands and laps free, legs crossed, and attention forward. So, it's vital your students have a cue for getting to this place and into position quickly. Here are some suggestions for your meeting cues:

- Put your arms out as if giving a huge tree trunk a hug
- Point to the meeting area and smile

- Motion for the students to get up, and push both arms toward the meeting area
- Simply stand up, look at the students and sit down at the area and wait for them to orderly file in

Choose one of these options you are comfortable with—or make up one of your own. As with the other cues, practice this many times. Be diligent in not speaking until all students are sitting down quietly, ready for the meeting, and be patient with the students who are slow to pick it up. Again, now is the time to work out the kinks in behavior. Finally, praise success immediately!

Get-Quiet Cue

Although a Green Light classroom is usually buzzing with activity, sometimes we will certainly need our students to be quiet. Introduce this cue by brainstorming with the students *why* you might need a get-quiet signal. Giving them the explanation behind the cue will help them to accept it. Next, model the cue you've chosen, then the desired reaction. Now let them practice—and make it fun! Ask students to talk loudly, nonstop, until you do the get-quiet cue. See how quickly they calm down and relax into silence. Possibly time how long it takes to get from your signal to absolute silence, and challenge them to improve on their time. Of course, as they learn to respond properly, praise them immediately, and ask them to praise each other. Here are some suggestions for get-quiet cues:

- Hold two fingers up in the air
- Hold hand up in the air, spreading out your five fingers
- Stand in a certain section of the room
- Hold one finger to your lips
- Hold hand up horizontally, and gradually chop it down

As with the silent class-meeting cue, choose one of these options you are comfortable with, or make up one of your own. Be sure your students have practiced this cue many times before you attempt to use it for real. No matter how frustrating it may seem, do not speak once you've made the cue. Once you say, "Hey guys, this is the quiet cue," the whole point of a silent cue is lost.

The Attention-Getter Cue

This cue uses no words. However, it is not quite silent. In a Green Light classroom, sometimes it is necessary to get attention quickly. To do this, you need some sort of noise maker. Once the students hear the noise, they are expected to stop what they are doing and pay attention. Explain this to your students then model it. Finally, have them practice it several times. Here are some suggestions for the attention-getter cue:

- Teacher claps three times, and then the students clap in response
- Teacher claps in a beat, and the students finish the beat
- Teacher snaps fingers on both hands until all students are paying attention
- Teacher shakes a can of beans or uses another noise-making instrument

Try to use these attention cues sparingly. If you snap your fingers all the time, for example, the effect will eventually wear off, and your students will become resentful.

Student Cues

Your *students* should also use silent cues. Silent cues can limit the volume in the classroom, and it can give students a powerful way to communicate. In a Green Light classroom, you need at least three essential silent student cues:

1. Always up;

2. I got it; and

3. I need to use the bathroom.

Always Up!

The prevalent attitude in a Green Light classroom is "Always up!" This means everyone in the room is committed to keeping a positive attitude. Because people occasionally forget to stay positive, you need a special "Always Up!" signal for both teachers and students to remind each other that, in this class, people are not negative. When introducing this silent cue, make the gesture, and ask the class to practice with you. Then, use a student volunteer to act out a quick skit demonstrating how to use it. For example, you could say to the student, "Well that's a *dumb* idea!" Then, when the student gives you the "Always up!" gesture, you immediately apologize and move on.

This cue is a simple but powerful device to short-circuit petty squabbles and keep the class on track. You can use it when students are negative about an activity or their work, and students can use it with each other when someone makes a mean remark. For example, Tori told Mary she has bad handwriting. Instead of retaliating, Tori gave her the "Always up!" signal, and Mary apologized. Once the class has grasped this cue, you'll find students using it with you.

I Got It!

The "I got it!" gesture is simply one thumb up with the hand close to the heart. This is simply a gesture that shows you the student understands the concept. This can be a quick, silent way for the student to communicate that he is ready to move on. When you see this gesture from several students, you know the class is getting the concept.

I Need to Use the Bathroom!

Here's a silent way for students to convey they need to leave the room to go to the bathroom: The student simply holds a hand up and crosses the pointer and middle finger. This saves you from unnecessary interruptions. When you see this, a simple nod will signal to the student they have permission to leave the room.

DAY 3: BUILDING THE CLASSROOM COMMUNITY

How Your Students Are Feeling

If the first two days have gone well, your students should be starting to get into the rhythm of their new classroom. They will be comfortably settling into daily routines, beginning to understand what is expected of them, and getting to know each other.

Your Goal

Today, the primary focus is on creating a strong sense of classroom community. By the end of the day, students should feel they are beginning to work together as a single unit, looking out for each other, and helping each other to succeed. They'll do this in three basic ways:

1. By understanding the issue of "acknowledgment" and the role it plays in the classroom—not only *how* it is done, but *how often* it is done;

2. By understanding the idea of "class jobs" and the role they play in developing and maintaining a high-performance team; and

3. By understanding the value of charting success—both privately as individuals and publicly as a group.

Why?

In a Green Light classroom, students need to function as an effective and efficient unit. For example, the signals and cues described in day two only work if every student follows along. Working as a unit requires constant encouragement—from the teacher, of course, but also from student to student. In addition, working together requires a clear sense of expectations, understanding what is required of everyone to maintain a truly successful learning environment. Finally, working together requires common goals, provided by the use of public, all-class success charts. How effectively these aspects of the classroom are handled often dictates the level of success students can attain, both as individuals and as a class.

How?

Suggested Schedule for Day Three

8:00–8:30:   **Welcome**

Give each student a high five as they walk into the room.

Play the song "I Can See Clearly Now."

Activity: Teams create a "team handshake," and they practice it several times.

8:30–9:00:   **P.E.** As demonstrated in day one, line up to "Pretty Woman."

9:00–9:30:   **Memory Pegs Practice**

Practice the Pegs as a class, in teams, and as pairs.

Teams present their new team handshakes to the class.

9:30–10:00:   **Acknowledgment Introduction**

Discuss "acknowledgment," its purpose, and how it will be used.

Teach students a variety of ways they can offer praise to each other.

Practice these types of acknowledgment.

10:00–10:30: **Class Mural**

All students work together to create a large mural.

10:30–11:00: **Class Jobs Introduction**

Discuss class jobs.

Assign class jobs.

11:00–11:30: **Graphing Introduction**

Explain why goal graphs are going to be used in many places in the classroom, both individually and as a class.

Explain the morning-attendance graph.

Team math activity—make a pizza graph.

11:00–11:30: Graphing Introduction

Explain why goal graphs are going to be used in many places in the classroom, both individually and as a class.

Explain the morning-attendance graph.

Team math activity—make a pizza graph.

11:30–12:00: Class Meeting

Students share what their goals are for this year.

12:00–1:00: Lunch

1:00–1:30: Learning Games—100-Square and Spelling Grids

1:30–2:00: Class Routines—check for understanding; ask if they have questions.

Students work together to review all class routines they have learned.

Give a short test on this topic. Set students up for success by making it quick and easy.

Practice graphing by charting the results of the entire class for this quiz.

2:00–2:30: Journal Reflection

Students write about their day.

2:30–2:35: Reset

Students clean up the room, then *hop* out the door to "Hit the Road Jack."

As you start day three, continue the routines of the first two days. For example, start the day with upbeat music as students walk into the classroom. Use the appropriate signals to begin, and perhaps even remind students of and quickly practice the various signals.

Acknowledgment Introduction

One of the primary goals for day three is that students learn about and understand the idea of *acknowledgment* or *praise*. Praising, complimenting, and acknowledging each other is a major part of class cohesiveness.

To introduce this idea, begin with a group discussion focusing on how it feels when someone gives them a compliment, or thanks them. Ask if they have enjoyed the way it has been done the first two days, and ask if they would enjoy having this be a regular part of every lesson, every day. Typically, students are universally enthusiastic about this idea. Clarify by saying that, in this classroom, acknowledgment is not just the teacher's job but is students' responsibility as well.

Explain there are a variety of ways students can show appreciation and recognize each other for their efforts. It can be done verbally, physically, or a combination of both. Discuss each way, providing specific examples.

For example, ask how they might thank each other *verbally*. They'll start with common phrases such as, "Well done" or, "That's great!" Now, invite them to expand these ideas and invent new and creative things they could use. Now, they might begin saying things such as, "Absolutely, totally awesome!" or, "You're a rock star, dude!" Based on this conversation, they begin to see that creativity is not only allowed in this classroom, it will be actively encouraged! As the year goes by, continue to allow them time to devise more and more playful, original verbal ways to acknowledge each other. In this way, as discussed in Principle 1: True Learning Communities: Students Taking Responsibility, they are now inventing their own forms of acknowledgment.

Repeat this process with a discussion about physical forms of acknowledgment, starting with the common ones, such as a handshake or a high five. Once again, challenge them to concoct alternative ways of physically acknowledging each other, such as "high threes" or "behind the back tens."

At this point, students should stand and repeatedly practice each form of acknowledgment—verbally, then physically, and then together.

Complete this introductory acknowledgment session by making three important points:

1. Explain that, in many situations, the best compliments are *specific*. For example, if Clarke used vibrant colors in his painting, then that should be specifically noted. Instead of simply saying, "Good job," the student giving the compliment could use more precise words, such as, "Clark, the colors you chose were perfect for your picture!"

2. Point out that, once everyone is into the rhythm of using acknowledgment frequently, you'll introduce them to even more ways of appreciating each other. For example, you'll show them some silent ways of praising, like a "golf clap" (silently tapping three fingers of one hand on to your other hand). Tell your students there are group ways of acknowledging each other, such as everyone getting up and dancing for 30 seconds. Let students know that more exciting acknowledgment options are coming!

3. Finally, clarify that they will be not only acknowledging each other for their success *but for their honest efforts as well*—even when those efforts might not be successful at first. Ask them why they might do this. Students quickly understand that honest effort leads to learning quickly and easily.

Class Mural

To reinforce praising as an important part of the classroom, introduce a cooperative activity—such as a class mural—where every student must participate for the activity to succeed (Mitra, 2008, pp. 20–25). Start the mural by taking one large piece of construction paper. Cut the piece of paper into big puzzle pieces, and give each student a piece to decorate. For the mural to work and be put back together again, all students must complete their parts of the puzzle. When all pieces have been returned, use masking tape to reassemble the mural on the wall. Another option might be to glue each puzzle piece to a magnet, and then reassemble the class mural on a metal surface.

Either way, once it is put together again, students can now praise other students for their contributions, being as specific as possible! This activity serves two main purposes: one, to physically display to students that success is not fully achieved unless *everyone* does his or her share; and two, to practice praising.

Class Jobs

After you have shown that we all must work together to achieve, you can expand that idea to their class jobs. For the class to work well together, all teams must work well together. And, for a team to work together well, everyone must know what is expected of them: what their job is within the team. Just as puzzle pieces fit together to form a complete puzzle, each job fits together to make a high-performing team.

It may take some brainstorming to find a class job for each student, but it can be done. Here are some suggestions for jobs:

- Greeter (when a visitor enters the room, the greeter is in charge of finding out what that person needs and greeting them)
- Attendance attendant (keeps track of attendance)
- Librarian (keeps track of the books)
- Mediator (helps resolve conflicts)
- Artist (draws on the board when the teacher needs it)
- Supplier of text books, as needed
- Supplier of supplies—such as pencils and paper, as needed
- Collector of supplies—gathers supplies at the end of each day
- Supply tidier—responsible for keeping the communal supply area tidy

An additional option is to give several students the same job; for example, it usually works well to have more than one sweeper.

Complete this discussion by working together and assigning each person a class job for today. Explain that this will only be their job for today—tomorrow they will switch jobs, so everyone can learn each of the class jobs.

Individual-Goal Graphs

Tell the students that at various times throughout the year they will be making graphs showing their progress in certain academic areas, such as reading, writing, history, or math. Explain the importance of seeing a visual image of their success, because this often helps them clearly understand how well they are doing in certain areas, and where they can improve. Also, if they happen to have one poor result, they can see this is just a slipup, not up to their usual standard.

Remember that this is only a *brief* discussion about and introduction to the idea of graphing their success. In a few moments, they will be having a more lengthy class conversation about class goals, and this is where much more understanding develops about the overall importance of charting their successes. There is no need to create individual graphs at this point; this will be part of their day-four activities.

Attendance Graphs

Explain to students that, when they come into the classroom every morning, there will be a creative way to find out who is here, which also allows them to practice their graphing skills. This will be a graph outline on the board with a title such as "Favorite Season," with each of the seasons listed. As they arrive, all students will mark their favorite season by writing their names under their favorite season. When class begins, using this information, students work in teams to create a bar graph or perhaps a pie chart. Practice this activity immediately by creating a four-column chart on the board, using topics such as "My favorite color" or "A country I'd like to visit." Invite all students to sign their names in one of the columns, and let them work together in their teams to create a graph showing this information.

Class Goals

After discussing acknowledgment and introducing class jobs, all your students should be rapidly developing a feeling of being an important part of the class. Given this foundation, it's time to introduce the idea of class goals. In your classroom setup, one bulletin board was left blank. Tell your students this is where graphs will be posted, charting everyone's progress on tests. Explain that success on a test is always a *class effort*.

This is a good time to mathematically illustrate how one extremely low grade will throw off the success of the whole group. Come up with a scenario where the rest of the class worked diligently and achieved high scores, but one student did not try and received a zero mark. Students will be amazed at how negatively that zero affects the final, averaged class score. End this discussion by explaining that only the *average* of all of the students' grades will be represented—this not only reminds students that they are working together as a class but also helps many students feel safer because their individual score will not be posted.

With the class, set a goal for the first test. Make sure the bar is set high but not so high that it will not be achieved. For example, you might organize a short test on class routines, with 10 questions, with the goal that the average number of correct answers for the whole class will be 80%.

Note: This first test is an opportunity to set the students up for success, *as it sets the tone for the entire year.* So, give them plenty of time to prepare, and encourage teamwork as they review what they have done so far. When the test is complete and has been checked, graph their performance. If you are comfortable with it, be overly dramatic, and make a huge show out of revealing the average test score. You want the students to roar with excitement when they see what they can achieve together.

When you begin to graph class performance on specific academic skills, consider using a *monthly bar graph* because it provides a striking visual of how well the class is progressing on a simple 100 scale. An example is shown in Figure 6.4.

Figure 6.4 Monthly Bar Graph

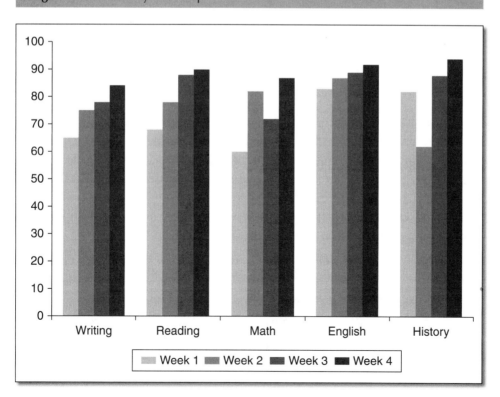

The bottom line is that you can teach a *perfect* lesson in *perfect* conditions; but, if a student simply is not invested in the process, if a student doesn't care, they absolutely will not perform. Simply put,

> *Student motivation is the key to class success.*

Therefore, now is the time to set the tone for success. Students should leave your classroom at the end of day three feeling like they are a part of something *big*. They should feel like they are each individually important to the group's achievements.

DAY 4: CREATING MULTIPLE ARENAS FOR SUCCESS

How Your Students Are Feeling

By day four, you should have a group of students taking rapid steps towards becoming a powerful learning team. Today's activities will offer students multiple opportunities to practice what they have learned so far—in terms of cues, signals, routines, acknowledgment, and graphing. Yet, the *format* of today's activities will open new doors of understanding by demonstrating multiple ways in which every student can achieve success. The first three days were highly focused on creating an optimistic, affirming, and encouraging classroom atmosphere. These new activities, conducted with the same general sense of excitement and celebration, will advance this general attitude of enthusiastic learning.

Your Goal

Think of the entire first week as a boot camp of *intensely positive situations*. Today will be a natural extension of this approach, where students will experience multiple levels of success. This time, however, the events will be divided into three distinct arenas of success: individual, small teams, and whole class. Students need to understand that learning and success can occur in multiple ways, on multiple levels—and all of them are going to play an important part in this classroom

Why?

So far, in the first three days, the majority of the learning has been done as a class or in small teams of three or four students. However, you have not yet made the clear distinction that *learning occurs on multiple levels*. When students understand what the different levels are, and that each way is just as important as another, you will have the freedom to adjust your teaching strategy to the one best suited to a particular unit or lesson.

How?

Suggested Schedule for Day Four

8:00–8:30:   Welcome

Give each student a high five as he or she walks into the room.

Play the song "I Can See Clearly Now."

Activity: Teams create team mascots.

8:30–9:00:   P.E. As demonstrated in day one, line up to "Pretty Woman."

9:00–9:30:   Memory Pegs Practice

Practice the Pegs as a class, in teams, and as pairs.

Teams present their mascots to the class. Use each presentation as an opportunity for the other students to practice various forms of acknowledgment.

9:30–10:00:   Attendance Graphs

In teams, make pie graphs from the attendance chart for today.

10:00–10:30: Read-Aloud Time

Suggested first book: *Thank You, Mr. Falker,* by Patricia Polacco.

Students form pairs and create a storyboard from the story.

Storyboards are shared and acknowledged.

10:30–11:00: Art Class

11:00–11:30: Individual and Team Success, and Graphing Practice

As individuals, students read and work out a humorous math problem.

Individually, they graph their results. Team members celebrate each other's success.

Teach a math review skill to the whole class. Teams work together on a team test, and then they chart and celebrate their success as a team.

11:30–12:00: Class Meeting

Students share what their favorite parts of this class have been so far.

12:00–1:00:   Lunch

1:00–1:30:   Learning Games—100-Square and Spelling Grids

(Continued)

(Continued)

1:30–2:00: Graphing Practice

Give a short quiz on the book *Thank You, Mr. Falker.*

Set the students up for success by making it quick and easy.

Graph it the results as a whole class.

2:00–2:30: Journal Reflection

Students write about their day.

2:30–2:35: Reset

Students clean up the room, and then they *hop* out the door to "Hit the Road Jack."

Team Mascot

The team mascot can be anything: a drawing of a character that includes interests from all members of the group, a real stuffed animal, or a puppet made by the team (these are created with brown paper lunch bags). If students make mascots, all team members must add at least one characteristic or feature to it. Throughout the school year, the mascot can reappear whenever needed to add spice, flavor, or excitement to any activity.

Read-Aloud Time

Read-aloud times occur frequently in a Green Light classroom—as they do in most classrooms. However, this is the first time students have encountered it this week, and the way it will be used may be slightly different from how they have experienced it in previous years.

Explain that you want them to be listening carefully to the story because they will be learning about it on several levels. Therefore, they should pay attention closely while you read the story because at the end of it you have a special activity waiting for them.

For this first story, consider using the book *Thank You, Mr. Falker* by Patricia Polacco. At the end of the story, invite students to work together to create a "storyboard" for what they heard. A storyboard is typically a sequence of five distinct events in the flow of a story:

1. Intro

2. Problem

3. Beginning

4. Middle

5. End (solution)

Invite students to work together in teams to create pictures of each of these events. When they are done, they can share what their team has created and, as always, acknowledge other teams for their work.

While this process can work quite successfully, and frequently captivates students' attention, another option to engage students in a story is to use a "Doodle-Predict" sheet. This unique approach to looking at a story helps many students understand it at a much deeper level than merely listening to it or reading it. For details on this idea, see Lesson Set 9 in Chapter 7 (pp. 150–153).

Arenas of Success

Today, students will have the opportunity to engage in an activity from each of these three distinct arenas of success: *individual, small team,* and *whole class.*

The Individual Arena of Success

Intrapersonal learners—students who learn best on their own—need to understand that they do have a place in this classroom. Some learners simply prefer to work alone. To acknowledge this type of learning style, set up a quick activity that requires little help from you or others. Let students work silently on it as individuals. This activity should only call for 10–15 minutes of sit-down time.

For example, use a humorous math story problem that ends with five basic questions. The story could be anything light and entertaining, to capture and hold student's attention; however, the problem itself would be quite simple to solve. Alternatively, give students a short story to read, where they become the detective and try to answer five questions to solve a mystery. It bears repeating: The key is that while the activity itself must be somewhat amusing and enjoyable for the students, it must also be geared to a level where all students can experience success.

It's important that the level of challenge in these activities be carefully considered. They must be fairly easy to complete, so all students can be successful. The goal is *not* to teach new content; instead, the primary focus—in fact the *only* focus—is that all students succeed.

To check the answers, give students a choice of checking them with a partner or team, or they can get an answer key and check on their own.

Once everyone in the class has succeeded, hand out an individual, notebook-sized graph. Ask your students to chart their progress on their own individual graph. An example of an individual graph for this type of activity is shown in Figure 6.5.

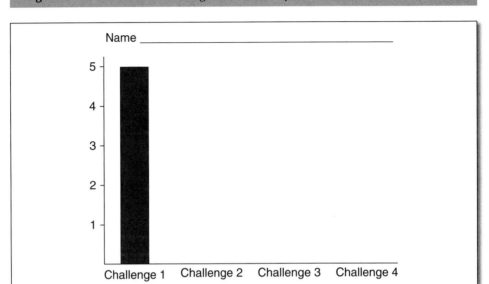

Figure 6.5   Individual Challenge Success Graph

Doing the activity, and graphing the results, serves several purposes, but the most important one is to let those introverted or intrapersonal learners know that you do have a place for them in the class, and they will be able to celebrate their *individual* success. Until now, most of the activities have been cooperative. Make sure you take a break from this style to let those students who prefer to work alone get their time. This does not mean hand out a worksheet and be done with it; graphing and praising should be the primary components in this process.

The Small-Team Arena of Success

Next, introduce a team-oriented activity where the team needs to meet a goal or beat a time deadline. For example, teach a math-review skill, one most students are likely to be familiar with from the previous year. Then, ask teams to practice it together, helping each other work out the correct answer. Finally, give them a team test where they are timed to see how rapidly they can work together to complete the test.

It is very important never to have the teams competing against each other. They should always be working toward a common goal. Never start with "The team with the best _____ wins." This is a recipe for discontent, disruption, and disaster. Instead, offer goals along the lines of, "Any team to finish within five minutes gets praise!" This way, teams are essentially challenging time and not each other.

You will soon find that teams start to encourage other teams once their team has made the goal. It's important to note that the "prize" for team accomplishment should rarely be candy or material items. Set the tone of simple praise and acknowledgment as a reward. If you start with material items as a reward, students will naturally start to expect more of these in the future. The reward structure should always be intrinsic (self-motivation) not extrinsic (what can I get for this?).

Note that this activity offers opportunities for teams to earn team points, as discussed on day one. Watch for the point-earning behaviors, and reward students liberally to develop their awareness of the importance of these behaviors and to reinforce this idea as something they should be observant about every day, during every activity—whenever they are working with their team.

The Whole-Class Arena of Success

Yesterday, the whole class experienced success on a test. The idea here is to anchor the theme of class success. Remember that the *routine* is important here: Explain why the test is relevant, set a goal as a class, take the test, check the answers, and end by *graphing the success.*

Today, the perfect opportunity has been created to reinforce this concept. In the morning, you read a book to the class during read-aloud time, followed by a storyboard opportunity with their teams. Based on this, students should be fairly familiar with the story. Now, after lunch, inform them that a "test" is coming about the story they heard in the morning. This test is important because being asked about something several hours later helps cement the ideas in their brains, a learning process they'll be using throughout the school year to maximize their success on *all* tests.

Invite them to sit together as a team and review what they remember about the story. After several minutes, ask if any team has a question about any of the characters, what order things happened in, or any other details from the story. When all questions have been answered, distribute a very short test to each student. When the tests are completed, check them, and work together to graph the results. Celebrate the success!

One of the less-obvious aspects of using this approach to tests—individual, small team, or whole class—deals with the emotional attitude students have towards tests in general. If your first few tests are arduous, students instantly form the perception that your tests are going to be too hard. So, there's a strong chance they might fail, and they will approach tests with negative emotions.

Instead, by approaching your first few tests in all three arenas of learning in this manner, you are actually training students to *look forward* to tests as being a chance to show off their skills and knowledge. Developing this attitude often takes patience and requires baby steps of success as you replace—or simply erase—bad thoughts and feelings towards tests students may have dragged in with them from previous school years. Therefore, if you have any of the traditional, lengthy, deadly-dull diagnostic tests often given to students at the start of the year, *avoid them with a passion!* Do whatever it takes to put them off until the second—or possibly even the third—week of school. Wait until students have developed a more positive and productive attitude toward taking tests. Right now, your primary focus is on smashing the myth that tests are necessary evils. Instead, the goal is that students see tests primarily as opportunities to *show what they know*, gain praise from others, and celebrate their victories!

DAY 5: DEVELOPING EXPECTATIONS, INCREASING CONFIDENCE, AND . . . *CELEBRATING!*

How Your Students Are Feeling

Think about what your students have gone through so far in this unique first week of school. They've learned unusual signals that help the classroom run faster and operate more efficiently, discovered they are smart on many different levels, and celebrated their own accomplishments as well as those of other class members. They've experienced success as an individual, within their small teams, and even as a whole class. They've played, laughed, and enjoyed themselves.

Now, think about what they *haven't* done. They haven't:

- Sat too long;
- Yawned in boredom;
- Had to be quiet for long periods of time;
- Felt stupid, frustrated, or stressed; or
- Experienced failure.

In other words, they've been experiencing an entirely different way to behave towards themselves, each other, and the teacher. Many students will actually be *excited* to come to school each morning, a rare and wonderful development!

Your Goal

This fifth and final day of this critical Five-by-Five week of school has been directly focused on developing *student confidence*. Therefore, it's vital your students walk away at the end of this final day feeling confident they will continue to:

- Be accepted by their peers;
- Be respected as an important contributor to the success of the class; and
- Experience high levels of success.

Putting a structure firmly in place that guarantees your students this process will continue is the key to ending on the highest note possible, and subsequently providing a powerful launching pad for the rest of the school year.

Why?

Because the start of the year has been so unusual, many students will now need to be assured that this experience has not been a setup. They need to see that, with their input and help, what they experience in their classroom really will continue to feel this way for the rest of the school year. In fact, they need to know things will not only continue to follow the path that has been set so far, but may actually get even better. And, perhaps most important, they need to see where this belief in their abilities can take them—to a level of success both personally and academically they may have never before believed possible.

How?

Suggested Schedule for Day Five

8:00–8:30:   **Welcome**

Give each student a high five as he or she walks into the room.

Play the song "I Can See Clearly Now."

Activity: Students form pairs or trios and create skits on inappropriate and appropriate behaviors for a successful classroom.

8:30–9:00:   **P.E.** As demonstrated in day one, line up to "Pretty Woman."

9:00–9:30:   **Memory Pegs Practice**

Practice the Pegs as a class, in teams, and as pairs.

Teams present their skits to the class.

Acknowledgment is practiced.

9:30–10:00:   **Class Meeting**

Students share what they think makes this class work smoothly.

(Continued)

(Continued)

10:00–10:30: "We Agree..." Poster

As a class, students create a "We Agree..." poster showing the agreements they will follow as a class.

All students sign the poster.

10:30–11:00: Music Class

11:00–11:30: Assignments Introduction

Explain the homework policy.

Create "brag books" where students will put their best work.

11:30–12:00: Class Meeting

Students share what their experience has been with homework.

12:00–1:00: Lunch

1:00–1:30: Learning Games—100-Square and Spelling Grids

1:30–2:00: Drop Everything and Read Time

2:00–2:30: Journal Reflection

Students write about their day.

2:30–2:35: Reset

Students clean up the room, and then they *hop* out the door at the end of the day to "Hit the Road Jack."

By day five, students have developed some very clear ideas about what to expect in your class. At the same time, you have begun to know the personality of the class as a whole through your morning greetings, brief personal conversations, class meetings, watching what choices they made, and watching how they interact with each other during activities.

Based on these observations, you have probably also identified certain characteristics that make each student unique. For example, you know who the pleasers are and who may temporarily fall off track during the year. Despite the varied personalities, all students should feel the same thing: "I am an important part of this class, and I care about what happens this year." So now is the perfect time to introduce the fairly common idea of class expectations, although in a fairly *uncommon* way.

Appropriate Behavior Skits

The overall success of a Green Light classroom depends on students understanding how to behave appropriately towards each other. However, simply because it's so important doesn't mean it has to be approached in a serious, stern, or depressing manner. Like many ideas students have learned in so far this week, understanding appropriate codes of conduct can begin with movement, involvement, and laughter, while still providing a useful background to learning the important concept.

Ask students to create and present two team skits: one that demonstrates inappropriate classroom behavior and another that demonstrates appropriate classroom behavior. Encourage them to use what they have been experiencing this week as the basis of their skits. When each skit is presented, briefly ask the class to identify the appropriate (and inappropriate) behaviors this team used in their skit. Keep the discussions short, and focus on students stating as clearly as possible the appropriate and inappropriate behaviors.

When all students have completed their skits, celebrate! Allow them to enjoy the laughter this activity usually creates. It's important to simply move on at this point to the next thing on the daily schedule. You'll return to this idea later; but for now, simply let it drift in the back of the students' minds.

Class Rules

Most teachers introduce class rules on the first day of school. When done this way, it's easy to see how these can be seen almost as a warning—that if you break one of these rules, you will face serious consequences. This means the motivation to behave is now extrinsic: "I have to follow the rules, but only because the *teacher* says so!"

In a Green Light classroom, the motivation to behave should primarily be internal, or intrinsic. Students should be able to understand for themselves why certain behaviors are acceptable while others are not. This is why it is so useful to wait to introduce the idea of class rules until the students have had a chance to *experience* what learning can be like in a radically different environment—one where mutual support and personal choice have played an important role.

Given their first four days of experiences along these lines, students should now be able to understand that class rules are not merely something the teacher imposes on them. Instead, these rules are things they have already been doing naturally and, if they continue to follow them for the rest of the year, will help ensure their classroom is one filled with encouragement, excitement, learning, and success. When they see the important role these play in the continued success of their dynamic classroom, they will instinctively *want* to make these agreements with each other and support each other in following them throughout the year.

To set class rules, begin by calling a class meeting. Let the students share about what they like about the class. You might hear things such as:

"We get to move a lot."

"We get to talk to each other."

"We listen to music."

"We have fun."

"We get to work in partners and teams."

"We get to choose who we want to work with."

Keep the conversation very positive. Remember to specifically acknowledge each student's contribution to the conversation, and thank each person for sharing and adding an important part to the discussion.

Next, ask students this question:

> *"What do you think are some ways we should behave to keep everyone feeling safe and learning together?"*

This discussion sets up the "rules" of the classroom. Come to agreement on the ones they think are most important, usually four or five. Ask a group of students to write these agreed-upon expectations on a large sheet of paper, and post them on the wall. When the list has been created, *ask each student to sign it.*

An important note: One of the keys to this strategy of having the students create the list of agreements is to avoid using negative "trigger" words, such as *don't* or *never*. Also, refrain from calling these agreements "rules." Some students, when they hear this word, will react and rebel against them purely out of instinct—they just hate rules! Instead, once the agreements have been created, perhaps simply write, "We Agree To . . ." at the top of the page.

The student investment in these "We Agree To . . ." items is priceless. It is amazing how quickly a student will correct his behavior when all you do is point to the agreement personally made by that student (Crowe, 2008, p. 44–47). Students are less likely to break their *own* rules than those arbitrarily handed down by the teacher.

Homework

In an elementary school Green Light classroom:

Homework is rarely ever assigned.

Many teachers may be startled by the idea of *not* relying heavily on homework as a primary teaching strategy; so, let's take a moment to clarify the reasons behind this suggestion. There is a significant amount of research suggesting homework should be assigned with great care—only in a specific set of circumstances, for very specific reasons. It is not appropriate to assign homework that covers sections not discussed in class, nor is it productive to give students "busywork," which is boring and makes students resentful. Thus, Green Light teachers do not set homework if it is unfair or unproductive.

They are also aware of the emotional importance of this issue.

Imagine a group of students at the end of the day. They are bopping out the door, happy for many reasons: They are on a high because of the upbeat music; they have learned new material and are confident they know it; and they are looking forward to doing things they love to do in their free time that evening.

Now, imagine a different group of students trudging out the door with backpacks full of books. They arrive home knowing they have two hours of homework—essentially busywork—to complete. As they grumble their way through this work, attempting to be good students, what do you think is happening to their attitude?

Ask yourself this question:

Which group of students would you rather teach?

In addition, think about how much anxiety a student must have if she goes home, looks at the homework worksheet and does not understand, then walks into class with the work incomplete. That student may well start out the day in an unenthusiastic or stressed mood. All she can think about is the consequences she will have to face for not having completed her homework. When students feel this way, teachable moments are rare indeed, and you may well lose a large chunk of valuable class time, all because of some essentially unnecessary busywork assigned for homework the previous night.

While homework assignments are rarely given to support lessons delivered in a Green Light classroom, they may *occasionally* be used. Homework assignments are only ever given to students for three specific purposes:

1. When students are expected to study for a test with very familiar terms;

2. When they are asked to do independent reading in a book they are already familiar with; and

3. When students specifically request extra practice on a concept, and when support is available at home.

In the first situation, if students are sent home with a set of familiar flash cards to practice a concept, they are very likely to complete the task with ease. This makes the use of the time at home valuable because it supports something that has *already been taught well.* After practice at home, which confirms how much this student knows about the topic, the next morning they will often be excited to show their skills on a test.

In the second situation, reading independently is always an important part of learning and growing as a reader. However, students should *already be familiar with the book,* and have started reading it in class, before taking it home to read on their own. This way, they are merely extending something in which they have already demonstrated their abilities. The task becomes merely a pleasurable extension of an area of competence rather than a solo venture into new territory, without support.

Finally, if a student struggles in a certain content area, in Green Light classrooms, students are usually comfortable asking for help. They are used to—and expect—success, so they usually turn to each other and the teacher to ask how they can reach their normal level of achievement. When students *ask* for additional help and support, their entire outlook towards homework is different: They are doing it because they *want to,* for a reason they understand and believe is *valid.* Still, even this situation can be potentially dangerous unless the proper support is available at home: Do they have someone to ask for help if they become stuck? Being locked overnight in a sense of failure ("I can't figure this out!") can quickly damage a student's overall sense of self-confidence. Therefore, even this strategy must be used cautiously.

Explain it! All this being said, you'll need to take some time in class to talk about your homework policy. When presenting it to your students, be sure to explain the reasons behind it in as much detail as possible. Students appreciate these explanations. For one thing, it acknowledges them as being important enough to include in important conversations and decisions. In addition, these insights into your thinking let them know you really are carefully considering how to teach them best, not just giving them "stuff to do."

Plan on taking 20 to 30 minutes for this conversation. Much like the conversation about classroom agreements, you might start by asking them about their previous experiences with homework. You'll usually hear some good stories and some bad ones. Then ask why they think other teachers give homework. After they've offered several reasons, you'll be in a perfect place to tell them about your reasons for doing it your way. You might say,

> *I would never give you homework about something you don't know, because you might end up getting stuck, or even practicing something the wrong way—and then it might be even harder to learn later! So, the only reason I ever give homework is to practice*

what I've already taught you, when I'm sure you can already do pretty well. So, if you know it, why would we even do it? Well, it's like being a basketball player who already knows how to shoot the ball but has to practice many, many time, so he can do it even better. So, I'll only give homework to you when I feel you're ready to practice it well. And remember, it's never, ever a punishment!

By having this type of conversation with the students, you are establishing yourself as a facilitator, not a dictator, and the students have become participants, not prisoners. You have an excellent chance of getting students' agreement and understanding about why homework is handled this way in your class when it is addressed this way (Marzano, Pickering, & Pollock, 2001).

Brag Books

Brag books provide students a place where they can show their best work, share awards or written acknowledgements, and collect anything that demonstrates how well they are doing. To explain this concept, first—if you have one—show your students your own *professional portfolio*, where you might keep your college transcripts or awards. Explain that a portfolio represents the best of you, so the students will use their brag books to show off their best writing and projects throughout the year.

A Five-by-Five Conclusion

Starting the school year this way, using the High-Five Principles over and over, sets the stage for student success in a variety of ways. The routines and behaviors you create establish the parameters within which an amazing world of learning can unfold. They set up positive classroom behaviors, they allow every student to experience success many times over, they craft a feeling of community and belonging, and they give your students something to look forward to.

At the same time, by the end of this week, your classroom behaviors will not be set in stone. Working with real students is hardly ever a case of "once and done." You'll doubtless need to revisit and review certain parts of your classroom procedures at various times throughout the year.

Don't be surprised by this. Adaptation and adjustment are a natural part of the process whenever working with *any* group of people, and a group of elementary students is no exception. Just know that, the stronger the foundation laid with your students during their Five-by-Five experience, the easier it will be to make the necessary changes and corrections so your classroom continues to be filled with excited, happy, and proud learners.

7

High-Five Lesson Sets

Combining Green Light Strategies and High-Five Principles Into Dynamic Lessons

LEARN TO READ... AND BE FREE FOREVER!

OVERVIEW

This section offers a series of lesson sets designed to teach a certain topic. These examples illustrate how to combine the Green Light strategies with the High-Five Principles to bring learning to life. All the lesson sets are presented in a five-day flow but can be easily adjusted to one- or two-day formats as needed. For clarity, each lesson ends by highlighting which strategies and principles are used.

LESSON SET 1: THE EDITING DOCTORS

The red light way of teaching editing skills is to give students endless worksheets with incorrect sentences ready to be corrected and turned in. The Green Light method turns this potentially deadly dull process into a playful metaphor, where students become "doctors" and treat "patients" who have become "ill." The patients, in this case, are paragraphs, and the illnesses they have are the things that need to be corrected, such as spelling, capitalization, and punctuation.

Materials: lab coats, 5 or 6 "sick" essays, highlighters and/or pencils, pre-SCRIPT-ion pad (see p. 125), clipboards, and x-rays (corrected paragraphs printed on a transparency)

Pre-SCRIPT-ion For Writing

Dr. _____ Edit

Name of Writing

_____

Type of Illness

Severed spelling

Capitalization cold

Run-on runny nose

Indentitus

Punctured punctuation

Tense tension

Seriousness of Illness: 1   2   3   4   5

Recommended Treatment _____

_____

_____

_____

_____

_____

_____

_____

_____

_____

_____

_____

_____

_____

_____

_____

Subject: Editing for Grammar and Punctuation

	What and Why	How

Day 1	Introduce the concept in a novel way to create interest and intrigue.	Say to your students, "We have an epidemic! There are so many sick essays around. We have to help them. As doctors, we need to diagnose, prescribe, and treat our patients. To diagnose the problem, we need to look for six main illnesses:
		
		    Severed spelling
		    Capitalization cold
		    Run-on runny noses
		    Indentitus
		    Punctured punctuation
		    Tense Tension
		
		Show your students an example and diagnose the problem, then write a pre-SCRIPT-ion highlighting what to fix. Finally, show how to treat or fix the problem. To see if the diagnosis was correct, hold up a transparency with the illnesses in the essay highlighted.*

	Students act it out.	Students put on lab coats and call each other doctor. They talk about the six main illnesses with a partner.
Day 2	Make the concept real.	Show a sick essay and a treated essay with "bandages" on it, making it real. (See the High-Five Toolkit, pp. 172–178, for examples.)
	Students practice in pairs or groups.	Students walk to five or six stations diagnosing, prescribing, and treating sick essays.
Day 3	Students retell the concept.	Students interview each other to see if they saved any "patients."
Day 4	Memorize the content.	Use the SCRIPT acronym to remember the possible illnesses.
Day 5	Test day! Prove they are successful learners!	Tape 11 short sick paragraphs to the walls around the room, each one numbered, and each with only one illness. Students walk around and choose 10 to diagnose and write a prescription. Evaluate the prescriptions for a 10/10 grade. Graph the results.
	Celebrate!	Play the song "Witch Doctor" to celebrate the end of the lesson and the grasping of the concept.

Adjustments for K–2: Use "sick" (misspelled) words that need to be "cured." Then, move on to sick sentences. Focus on S-spacing (two fingers between each word), C-capital letter in the beginning, and a period at the end. For grades one and two, only focus on spelling and capitalization for sentences at first and move on to punctuation. Instead of an acrostic, use a physical memory strategy to remember spelling, capitalization, and punctuation. For example, they can stand on their tip-toes to remember capitalization.

If younger students have not yet developed letter awareness, acronyms obviously won't work for them. As an alternative memory device, consider using a popsicle stick/tongue depressor with memory cues written on it. Each student could be given a popsicle stick with a capital letter C at the top to remind them to check for capitalization, and a period at the bottom to remind them to check for punctuation. The popsicle stick itself might even be placed between words to act as a reminder to leave enough space between words. Also, the tongue depressor is a doctor's tool, so it ties in perfectly with the theme of being doctors.

Green Light Strategies Used

- *Memory*—Students use the acronym, SCRIPT.
- *Movement*—Students are moving around the classroom, checking the various paragraphs. During the majority of the lesson, they are in motion.
- *Novelty*—The whole process is unusual and exciting!
- *Socialization*—Students are working in groups as they diagnose the paragraphs.
- *Drama*—Students are dressing up as doctors.

High-Five Principles Used

1. *True Learning Communities*—Students are not just being told the information; they are taking responsibility for their learning as they work together to analyze the paragraphs, looking for illnesses.

2. *Working Within Their World*—The essays are more engaging if they have relevant or humorous content. Instead of having to work on dry, uninteresting content, the lesson succeeds because it draws students into the content while they simultaneously learn about the editing process.

4. *Learning Beyond Listening*—Students are not merely sitting and listening; they are engaged at multiple levels, up and moving as they become doctors, talk to each other, and check their diagnoses.

5. *The Learning Spiral*—Students are given the chance to practice with clear examples first and then verify their results. This will provide the foundation of understanding when they later make the step up to analyzing their own paragraphs and essays.

LESSON SET 2: THE GENIE-IN-THE-BOTTLE

The red light method of teaching the scientific method is to give students a diagram or worksheet showing the five basic steps of the scientific method—problem, hypothesis, test, results, and conclusion—and expect students to memorize it using rote rehearsal. The Green Light method involves magic, movement, and a hands-on experience! Instead of trying to memorize information to which they have no connection or understanding, students learn about the *scientific* method using the *discovery* method[3].

Materials: Two Erlenmeyer flasks, a rubber bouncy ball, pencil, paperclip, string, ribbon, masking tape

To prepare: cover the flasks with the masking tape, so they are opaque, masking the insides of the flasks. Gently squeeze the rubber bouncy ball into one of the flasks; dish soap can sometime help slide the ball in safely. Now, decorate the two beakers with creative—or mysterious!—symbols, hieroglyphics, or other markings. *Make the designs on the two flasks match each other as closely as possible.* Finally, use scotch tape to attach the paperclip to the eraser end of the pencil, with part of it sticking out, like a small hook. Now, you are ready for the lesson!

Subject: The Scientific Method

	What and Why	How
Day 1	Introduce the concept with a story and a magic trick!	*(Direct the students to sit around as you tell them this story.)* "I recently went on a trip to Egypt and was able to purchase a great souvenir—a real genie in a bottle." *(Hold up a flask with the rubber ball in it, although students don't know about the rubber ball!)* "This genie will hold onto anything as long as you ask it nicely. Watch, here's how it works." *(Stick the pencil into the flask. Tilt the flask so the bottom is sticking up into the air. Speak into the bottle)* "Oh Genie in the bottle, please hold onto the pencil!" *(When you tilted the flask bottom up, the ball will have rolled down near the opening. Tug gently on the pencil, to lodge it into place. Turn the flask over, maintaining tension on the pencil. Finally, release the flask and only hold the pencil: The flask appears to be hanging onto the pencil! Let students see this, then remove the pencil.)* "See, it's magic!" *(At this point, students will notice the paperclip, and typically shout . . .)* "No, it's just that paperclip—I bet you just hooked it on something!" *(Appear surprised!)*

What and Why	How
	"Oh, you noticed that? OK, so we have a problem: *You don't think there's a genie in this bottle! And your guess—your* hypothesis—*is that I'm just hooking this on something. Well, the only way to find out if a guess is right is to run a* test!*" (Repeat the same demonstration, using the other end of the pencil this time, which has no paper clip attached to it. It will still work, and students will be startled!)*
	"OK, so we had a problem: *You didn't think it was a genie. Then we developed a* hypothesis—*the paper clip had something to do with it! So we ran a* test: *We tried the other end of the pencil, the one without the paper clip. And what was the* result? *The bottle still stuck. So what's your* conclusion? *Well, if you don't think there really is a genie in this bottle, then we have to go back and develop a new* hypothesis!*"*
	*(Students' next guess is usually that there's some sticky tack, or glue, in the bottle that you're just jamming the pencil into. Repeat the experiment again, this time using string—and be sure to reinforce the key words—*problem *(sometimes called the 'question'),* hypothesis, test *(sometimes called the 'procedure');* results, *and* conclusion.*)*
	(Do two or three more tests, using different objects, such as the piece of ribbon, or a twig from a tree. Finally . . . explain to the students that they just went through the steps of a scientific process. They just conducted an experiment and didn't realize it. Then explain each step of the process:
	Problem—*What is holding onto items?*
	Hypothesis—*The paperclip is hooking onto something in the bottle.*
	Test—*Stick the other end of the pencil into the magic bottle to see what happens.*
	Results—*The pencil still sticks!*
	Conclusion—*There is a genie in that bottle! Or, at least, something they haven't yet discovered, which makes this work!*
	(For clarity, repeat these same five steps with each item, such as the string, ribbon, or twig.)

(Continued)

	What and Why	How
	Students act it out.	*Students practice an action with every step.* Problem—*Scratch the top of your head.* Hypothesis—*Rub your chin as if your are thinking.* Test—*Step in place firmly, saying, "Test, test, we must test!"* Results—*Bring your hands up to your eyes to make fake binoculars.* Conclusion—*Mime writing on a pad, then fold your arms.*
Day 2	Make the concept real.	*Demonstrate again, sticking even more items in the bottle, and show how each time the genie holds onto them.*
	Students practice in pairs or groups.	*Students plan how they would run their own experiment, outlining each step, as they seek to discover what makes this work!* *Once they have done this, students are now ready to be introduced to the two important aspects of running a test:* the independent variables *and the* constants. *Explain that the independent variables are the things that change, such as the pencil or string; the constants are the things that stay constant, such as the magic bottle.*
Day 3	Students retell the concept to show understanding.	*Students make a fake newscast covering the magic show. In groups of three or four, they create a sensational story exposing that we have genies and explain each step of the experiment.*
Day 4	Students memorize the content.	*Use the physical motions to remember the steps.*
Day 5	Test day! Prove they are successful learners!	*Hand students a written description of an experiment in paragraph narrative form. Students then use different colored highlighters to identify the five different steps of the scientific method in the paragraph. Graph the results.*
	Celebrate!	*Finally, they'll all want to know how it's done! But—as much as you might be tempted—don't give away the secret! That might spoil it for next year! Instead, secretly swap the flask with the ball in it for the one without a ball. Show students this flask, and allow them to hold it. Play "Do You Believe in Magic?" as students take turns looking in the empty flask and trying to make it work. It won't, of course! End by saying, "The genie only works for me!"*

Adjustments for K–2: Start with the genie in the bottle experiment, but only focus on problem, hypothesis, and test. It's more important that students grasp the concept of *questioning* and *experimenting*, rather than specific terms.

As K–2 students are limited in their writing skills, use a comic-frame format to show the sequencing of the steps. It allows them to show their knowledge through illustrations as well as through short captions. A testing alternative is to give students a set of cards depicting the steps for them to sequence. They can glue the picture down and write short captions to show their knowledge.

Green Light Strategies Used

- *Memory*—Actions are used to remember each of the five steps.
- *Novelty*—The use of a magic trick!
- *Tone*—The lyrics of the song "Do You Believe in Magic?" matches the lesson content.
- *Emotions*—Students will be fascinated, curious, and intrigued while trying to figure out how the magic bottle works. These emotions are key to getting students to engage fully.
- *Socialization*—Students are talking to each other often throughout this lesson as they try to figure out how it works.
- *Drama*—The story of the Genie in the bottle engages the students and gets them curious.
- *Visuals*—The creatively decorated flask creates a natural level of interest and draws in students' attention.

High-Five Principles Used

3. *Teach to the Moment*—Students love magic tricks, and as this is woven throughout the five days, they will be constantly focusing and refocusing on the lesson as they try to work out what is happening.

4. *Learning Beyond Listening*—Students are highly engaged in guessing what makes the magic bottle work—very different from just listening. They are also physically engaged when they do motions and link actions to the five basic steps of the scientific method.

5. *The Learning Spiral*—Each day, with each new angle that is taken to explore this content, the students are spiraling upwards in their ability to remember the five steps. They are gradually building a solid foundation upon which to remember the steps as they explore the idea from multiple angles. The spiral is also in evidence when they first learn the five basic steps of the scientific method; and only after they are familiar with these terms, on Day Two, are they introduced to additional new vocabulary, the independent variables, and the constants. Their understanding expands as their confidence spirals upwards.

LESSON SET 3: THE EDIBLE CELLS

The red light method of teaching about plant and animal cells is to show a diagram of each, and then hand students a worksheet of the same diagrams, missing its labels, for them to fill in the correct words. In a Green Light classroom, using the High-Five Principles, students create their own cells, carefully constructing each component, and then . . . they *eat* it!

Materials: candy necklace, licorice rope, green jellybeans, red jellybeans, miniature peanut butter cups, M&M's, miniature chocolate bars, plain sugar cookie mix, white icing, wax paper, onion skin, microscope

To prepare: To create the animal cells, first bake (or buy!) some large, *round* cookies. The licorice rope will become the cell membrane; the icing, the cytoplasm; the miniature peanut butter cup, the nucleus; the M&M's, the vacuoles; and the red jellybeans, the mitochondria.

To create the plant cells, bake (or buy!) some large, *square* cookies. The licorice rope will become the cell membrane; the icing, the cytoplasm; the miniature peanut butter cup, the nucleus; the miniature chocolate bar, the large vacuole; and the red jellybeans, the mitochondria. You can also add the green jellybeans for the chloroplasts and the candy necklace as the cell wall (you could also use long fruit roll-up snacks for the wall).

Subject: Plant and Animal Cells

	What and Why	How
Day 1	Introduce the concept with examples from their world.	Say to your students, "How many of you have eaten the ice cream that comes as tiny little dots that burst in your mouth? When you look at it, you can't believe that it will taste like ice cream, but all of those tiny little dots have to come together to make the complete cup of ice cream. Yeah, Dipping Dots are cool!
		Also, if you look at a hill of sand closely and take a handful of it, you can see that it is made of many little grains of sand put together to make that big hill.
		Well, every living thing is made of tiny little parts. Parts so tiny that we cannot see them with our eyes. We would need a microscope to see these tiny parts. These parts are called cells.
		Plants have a certain type of cell, and animals have another."
	Students draw the concept.	Students draw a beach scene using an impressionist method of tiny little dots making each living thing in the picture. The plants are drawn using tiny, little rectangular boxes. The animals are drawn using tiny, little circles.

	What and Why	How
Day 2	Make the concept real.	Show a slide of an onion skin under a microscope, and point out all of the parts of the plant cell. To assist students in identifying different parts, assign each one a job: *Cell Wall: The protector* *Cell Membrane: Doorman* *Mitochondria: Hard workers, converting energy* *Nucleus: The boss* *Vacuole: Storage* *Chloroplast: Makes the food* *Cytoplasm: Holds everything together*
	Students practice in pairs or groups.	*In pairs, students make an edible model of each type of cell using the materials stated above. Students end by eating their cells!*
Day 3	Students retell the concept to show understanding.	*Students again make a cell cookie. They now give their cells names and proceed to introduce each cell to other students. For example: "Here is Bob, an animal cell from a cat's paw; here is his nucleus—the boss of the operation; and, here is his cytoplasm." They end this lesson by—once again—getting to eat their cells!*
Day 4	Show the students how to memorize the content.	*Because each item has a job, you can connect an action to each job. For example:* *Cell Wall, the protector: Make a bicep muscle.* *Cell Membrane, doorman: Hold an imaginary door open.* *Mitochondria, hard workers converting energy: Swing an imaginary axe.* *Nucleus, the boss: wag your finger.* *Vacuole, storage: Make a motion like hugging a big tree to gather and store the needed supplies.* *Chloroplast, makes the food: Act like you're eating a sandwich.* *Cytoplasm, holds everything together: Interlock your hands, and clench them tightly.*

(Continued)

(Continued)

	What and Why	How
Day 5	Test day! Prove they are successful learners!	*Assignment: "Describe your family or school in a paragraph, and draw a picture representing your work."* *Students describe their family or school as a plant cell. Who would have which job?* *For example: "My mom would be the chloroplast because she makes all of the food." Or, "My principal would be the nucleus because he's the boss of the school." Or, "Our security guard would be the cell membrane because she lets people in and out of the school building."*
	Celebrate!	*To celebrate their success, students again get to create a cell cookie to lock in the learning. As they eat their plant and animal cells, they can continue to identify the various parts of a cell by saying things such as, "Oh my, this nucleus is mighty tasty!"*

Adjustments for K–2: Start with the impressionist drawings. Focus on the fact that all living things are made of cells. If they make the edible cells, just make the cell membrane, cytoplasm, and nucleus. Instead of writing a paragraph for the assessment, they can draw a picture (Tomlinson, 1999, p. 16).

Alternatively, the focus of the learning could be on the *shape* of the cells, as well as the essential parts. For assessment, give students paper pieces to cut and assemble making one-inch square or circle cells (cutting develops fine motor skill and shape recognition) while including each part. Then, the whole class could glue their cells into the outline of a flower (square cells) or dog outline (circle cells).

Green Light Strategies Used

- *Memory*—Students will readily recall making their cell cookies and use this as the primary way to remember the information.
- *Connections*—The teacher's opening discussion of the ice cream dots and the sand dune will help students understand the underlying idea that a seemingly large thing is actually made up of many smaller things.

- *Movement*—Students will move many times, such as when making their cookies, looking in the microscope, doing the memory movements for each job, or when introducing their cell cookie to other students.
- *Novelty*—Making the cell cookies will be unusual, but eating them will be *really* unusual!
- *Emotions*—Students will often laugh and smile when making their cell cookies.
- *Socialization*—Students are talking often in this lesson, sometimes directly about the content and other times merely socially chatting with each other.
- *Drama*—Introducing their cell to other cells will give some students the opportunity to utilize their dramatic and creative talents.
- *Visuals*—The cell cookie is a highly memorable visual aid.

High-Five Principles Used

1. *True Learning Communities*—Students are working together to help each other make their cell cookies, and doing this will be reinforcing the content as they discuss each part.

3. *Teach to the Moment*—Students love to eat anything, but especially cookies! This, more than anything else, will draw them in at the start of the lesson and engage them in the content.

4. *Learning Beyond Listening*—Students are learning by making their cell cookies, by talking to each other, by introducing their cookies, and by linking each part of the cell to a specific movement.

5. *The Learning Spiral*—Students are building success on success as they make three cookies throughout the week and as they experience the content in a wide variety of ways.

LESSON SET 4: ONE BIG KISS

The red light method of teaching the inference strategy in reading is with students reading paragraphs and answering multiple-choice questions where they need to infer the correct answer. The Green Light method involves movement, memory, and laughter! Individual worksheets are replaced with cooperative group charts, and students learn a "KISS" strategy while eating a Hershey's Kiss.

Materials: a bag of Hershey's Kisses, KISS chart poster, highlighters, five or six paragraphs that contain good material from which students can make inferences.

Subject: Making Inferences

	What and Why	How
Day 1	Introduce the concept with humor and a familiar connection.	Say to your students, *"Put your pinky in the air if you have an aunt or grandma who always wants to give you a big fat kiss when she sees you? How many of you try to run away"* (Laughter usually follows . . .)
		"Well, today I will be giving you a kiss that just might change your life! (Students usually say things such as, "Ewww, gross!" as they all laugh.)
		"Well, actually, we will really be kissing paragraphs!"
		Explain each step of the KISS method of inference:
		K: Key words *underlined.*
		I: Infer *using the clues.*
		S: Support *the inference with a reason.*
		S: Summarize.
	Students *talk* about each step then *act out* each step.	*First, students simply tell each other the four steps; ask them to repeat this several times.*
		Next, students act out each step:
		K—Key words *underlined: Dramatically underline a big word.*
		I—Infer *using the clues: Look through a magnifying glass.*
		S—Support *the inference with a reason: Cup both hands, and bring them up in the air, as if offering support.*
		S—Summarize: *Make "jazz hands": Hold your hands turned palm up, with elbows tucked in, and wiggling your fingers.*
		Practice this several times. Then play the song "The Shoop Shoop Song" (AKA "It's in His Kiss") by Betty Everett or "Sugar, Sugar" by The Archies as you pass out Hershey's Kisses to the students while they continue to practice KISS.
Day 2	Make the concept real.	*Preface this class example by telling the students, "I am going to walk into the classroom. Pay attention to the key things that happen."*
		Leave the classroom, and then walk back in, saying, "I can't believe this! Ooh, it's all just too much!"

	What and Why	How
		and slam down a book angrily. Ask your students to identify the key words *you used then identify the clues, such as the look on your face. Lead the discussion until they* infer *from the situation that you are angry about something. Finally, ask students to work with a partner to summarize what happened. If time allows, share the summaries with the class.*
	Students practice in pairs or groups.	*Post five or six paragraphs on the walls in different locations around the room. In pairs or trios, students work together to practice the KISS strategy on each paragraph.*
Day 3	Students retell the concept to show understanding.	*Students "teach" each other how to do the KISS strategy using the story of* The Three Little Pigs. *One student reads it out loud as the other student points out ways to infer. They both see how many times they can KISS the story.*
Day 4	Actively memorize the content.	*Use the KISS acrostic to remember the steps. Students should act out the motions several times, with different partners and groups, until everyone has memorized the steps.*
Day 5	Test day! Prove they are successful learners!	*Put five paragraphs on a sheet. Students choose four of the paragraphs and demonstrate how to use the KISS strategy to make inferences. First, they underline the key words. Then, in a space provided after each paragraph, they write down their inference and summary. Graph the results!*
	Celebrate!	*Again, play the song "It's in His Kiss" or "Sugar, Sugar" as you pass out Hershey's Kisses to the students while they demonstrate the KISS strategy again.*

Adjustments for K–2: Instead of using paragraphs, consider using pictures of community members wearing stereotypical outfits. Students would *infer* their occupation by circling the physical clues that indicate their jobs (chef hat, apron, cooking utensils). For assessment, place bags around the room with three or four related items in each bag. (For example, Bag 1 would have clues in the form of a leash, a bone, and a collar: Students would infer a dog). Students have to analyze the *"Klues," Infer* how they are related, *Support* their inference by telling what the objects are used for, and *Summarize* by drawing a picture that shows all the items being used.

Green Light Strategies Used

- *Memory*—Motions are used to memorize each of the four parts of the KISS strategy. The sentence is also a memory aid, called an acrostic.
- *Connection*—The early connection of getting a kiss from a relative is made, as well as how they are going to learn to "kiss" paragraphs.
- *Movement*—In addition to the memory motions, students are moving around the room as they look at the different paragraphs and use the KISS method of inference.
- *Novelty*—The use of Hershey Kisses!
- *Tone*—The lesson involves playing songs that match the idea of kiss.
- *Emotions*—Students have fun and laugh when making the KISS connection to a kiss they've received from a relative or when pretending to kiss each other.
- *Socialization*—Students are working in pairs on *The Three Little Pigs* story, and students are working in groups as they walk around the room talking about the paragraphs posted on the wall.
- *Visuals*—The lesson uses paragraphs hung on the walls.

High-Five Principles Used

1. *True Learning Communities*—Students are helping each other learn, working together in different formats.

2. *Optimum Learning Conditions*—Students feel safe because they have a clear acronym to work with when remembering the steps.

3. *Teach to the Moment*—All students remember getting one of *those* kisses; so, the lesson begins on a powerful note, with something that's real within their world.

4. *Learning Beyond Listening*—Students are linking the learning to movements.

5. *The Learning Spiral*—Students first learn the basic acronym, and they practice in multiple group settings, only moving forward when they are successful. Only at the end will they branch off to demonstrate this skill on their own.

LESSON SET 5: THE ANGLE TANGLE!

The red light method of teaching obtuse, acute, and right angles is to show the angles in a diagram or worksheet, and have students match them or pick them out in a multiple choice activity. The Green Light method involves movement and drama.

Materials: templates for drawing acute, obtuse, and right angles, and room to move!

Subject: Learning About Angles

	What and Why	How
Day 1	Introduce the concept with a story.	*Tell this story: "There was a cute (cup your hands in an acute angle) little puppy who lived in a house that was just right" (make a right angle with one arm straight up and the other out to the side). "He stumbled around because he was small. Eventually, a huge monster named Bob Tooth (stick one arm to the side and put the other arm almost completely on the other side, making an obtuse angle) found him. He was about to eat the puppy with his large jaws when he saw how adorable and sweet the puppy was and said, 'Aw you're a cute one!'"* *Now, explain what an acute, an obtuse, and a right angle are, and where they are in the story.*
	Students talk about it or act it out.	*Students act out each part of the story and tell it to each other. Invite them to exaggerate each of the angles when they appear in the story, to make certain they can identify each one.*
Day 2	Make the concept real.	*Give students templates with which to draw an acute angle for the dog's head, an obtuse angle for the monster's head, and a right angle for the dog's house. Students draw a picture of the events in the story.*
	Students practice in pairs or groups.	*In pairs, students walk around showing off their angle pictures. Play instrumental music in the background as you do this.*
Day 3	Students retell the concept to show understanding.	*Students physically make each angle with their arms as they tell the story. Then, ask some students to walk around the room making angles while the other students try to guess what angle they are making.*
Day 4	Students cement their understanding of the content.	*Students retell the story to each other in pairs, and they act out the angles, exaggerating the motions and clearly saying the actual name of the angle this time, such as saying, "the monster 'Obtuse'" instead of "Bob Tooth."*
Day 5	Test day! Prove they are successful learners!	*Place four pictures of each of the three types of angles randomly around the classroom, numbered 1 through 12. Tell students they must find two of each type of angle and write down the corresponding numbers. For example, they might find two right angles, and write down 7 and 10 on their paper by the words "Right Angles: _____, _____."*
	Celebrate!	*Play the song "The Right Stuff" by New Kids on the Block as students move randomly around the room. When the music stops, students get to make an angle with their bodies. Repeat over and over.*

Adjustments for K–2: You can teach this strategy as it is. The assessment might be a matching game instead of asking the students to write the words out.

Green Light Strategies Used

- *Memory*—The use of the story recalls the three different angles.
- *Movement*—The students act out the story, show each other their pictures, and walk around the room checking out the angles during the assessment.
- *Novelty*—The lesson uses a funny, weird story!
- *Tone*—The lesson uses music while students are walking around practicing the story, and the lesson uses music for the celebration, as the students walk around the room and stop to form an angle with their bodies as the music stops.
- *Emotions*—The lesson uses laughter, with the funny story, and the students enjoy making angles with their bodies.
- *Socialization*—Students work in pairs and groups many times during the week.
- *Drama*—Students get to act out the story, and they get to act out the angles!
- *Visuals*—Creating their own pictures of the story helps to reinforce the learning for visual learners.

High-Five Principles Used

1. *True Learning Communities*—Students are helping each other learn, as they show how to make the angles and comment on each other's pictures.

2. *Optimum Learning Conditions*—Students are learning at an easy, natural pace, and they are never threatened or challenged as the lesson is progressively reinforced.

3. *Teach to the Moment*—Students enjoy stories, especially when they are humorous.

4. *Learning Beyond Listening*—Students are linking the learning to specific actions.

5. *The Learning Spiral*—Students are learning in short, distinct steps as they move gradually from one successful challenge to another.

LESSON SET 6: THE LIVING TIMELINE

The red light method of teaching important dates in history, and the events we remember them for, is to have students read a textbook and make notes about the dates and those important historical events. Students then attempt to remember these dates merely by rote rehearsal. The Green Light method involves the use of drama, novelty, laughter, and ultimately—success.

Materials: paper and costumes

Subject: Historical Timelines

	What and Why	How
Day 1	Introduce the concept with an engaging conversation.	Say to your students, "How many of you have seen movies where someone goes back in time? Wouldn't it be interesting if we could go back in time? What would you do? What kind of people do you think lived at this time in history?"
	Students discuss time travel with each other, and then act it out.	Students pretend they are on a time machine and go back to the time covered in the unit of study. In groups of four or five, they choose a year to go back to and act out what they think would happen if they landed in that year.
Day 2	Make the concept real.	Show a clip from a movie that talks about time travel, perhaps Back to the Future. After the clip, ask students what they think it would be like to be stuck back in that time. In the discussion, introduce as many specific things that were really happening at that time in history.
	Students practice in pairs or groups.	Post five or six important dates around the room on sheets of paper. For example, for a unit on the American Revolution, you might pick 1776, 1778, or 1783. At each station, small groups of students have 5 minutes to pick out an important event that occurred that year (which you've already discussed in class). Students then act out this event for each other. Then, rotate to the next station and do the same thing, continuing until all groups have been to all stations.
Day 3	Students retell the concept to show understanding.	In pairs, students talk about what they were doing yesterday, what years they visited, and what the related important events were. Then, students individually create a timeline for these five or six events, using both pictures and words, showing the order of the events. Play music in the background as they work. At the end, students share their drawings and compliment each other's work.

(Continued)

(Continued)

	What and Why	How
Day 4	Show the students how to memorize the content.	*Pick one of the key events discussed so far, and create a rhyme that mentions both the date and the event. For example, in 1783, the Treaty of Paris was signed, officially ending the American Revolutionary War. You might say, "In seventeen hundred eighty-three, both sides signed a peace treaty. Written in Paris, France, they say, England and the patriots ceased fire that day." The whole class should practice this rhyme several times; then, create another rhyme together, using another event. Now, have students work in to teams to create rhymes that fit the other events. Teams then present their rhymes to the rest of class.*
Day 5	Test day! Prove they are successful learners!	*Students can be assessed in various ways for this lesson. They might draw a timeline showing the sequence of events. Or, they could write down the rhymes from these events, again, in some way demonstrating their knowledge about the order. Or, if time permits, students might even be able to individually act out these events for this timeline for their assessment.*
	Celebrate!	*After students perform well on the test, graph their successes, and display these successes for everyone to see and enjoy. You might also have them celebrate by creating a large "class timeline." This could be one large line going across the classroom, and groups of students stand somewhere on the line, each group representing one of the events.*

Adjustments for K–2: Actual dates aren't relevant yet to the majority of K–2 students, as they are still developing a concept of past, present, and future. For this age group, adapt the timeline to focus on *months* or *seasons*. For example, on Day 2, ask students to sort through activity cards (skiing, swimming, baseball) and choose which ones would best fit each month or season.

Green Light Strategies Used

- *Memory*—The use of the rhyme, every time, will help students remember the important events—and that would be fine!

- *Connections*—By discussing the idea of time travel and talking about what it must have been like to live at a particular period in time, history comes alive for students. Who hasn't dreamed of becoming a time traveler?
- *Movement*—The use of the stations keeps students moving. Acting out the various events also keeps their bodies in motion!
- *Novelty*—The time-travel conversation will keep students thoroughly intrigued.
- *Tone*—The use of music while drawing helps focus students' attention. The use of a rhyme as the primary memory device will be very helpful to auditory learners.
- *Socialization*—Students are working together in a variety of ways; and in every situation, they are talking to each other.
- *Drama*—Having the chance to act out the events that occurred at each year will be a source of great amusement to students, keeping them engaged and focused as they learn and remember.
- *Visuals*—The opportunity to draw out the timelines will help visual learners. The chance to act out each event also will serve as a strong visual device for learning and remembering the key ideas.

High-Five Principles Used

1. *True Learning Communities*—Students are not merely being told the key events related to each year. They are helping each other remember these events, working together to prompt each other and help each other learn.

2. *Optimum Learning Conditions*—Students will feel safe and secure in learning about timelines in multiple ways, by talking, acting, drawing, and rhyming.

3. *Teach to the Moment*—The opening of this lesson can be adapted to whatever might currently be of interest to the students. If there's a current movie that is popular, that takes place sometime in the past, this could be a wonderful starting point for the time-travel conversation.

4. *Learning Beyond Listening*—The rhymes, the drawings, and the conversations are all creative ways for students to link the learning to a specific memory trigger.

5. *The Learning Spiral*—In this lesson, students jump from success to success. They start with the conversation about the historical event. Once they are sure they all know it, they act it out successfully because anything can be right! Getting compliments for their drawings acknowledges another level of success.

LESSON SET 7: WRITING: GROSS GRAMMAR

The red light method of teaching grammar is for students to complete mountains of worksheets and spend endless days diagramming sentences. The Green Light method involves movement, memory, and laughter! Individual worksheets are replaced with cooperative group charts, and students get a chance to laugh.

Materials: chocolate chip or oatmeal raisin cookies, chart paper, markers, and index cards

Subject: Grammar

	What and Why	How
Day 1	Introduce the concept with fun and excitement as students earn cookies!	*Write the following sentence on the board:* "Cindy baked cookies." (Insert your own name!) *Keep the plate of cookies where the class can see them. Invite one student to come up and point to a noun in the sentence (Cindy, cookies). Give the student a high five for answering it correctly and give her a cookie as a reward. Do this again with another student as he points out the verb in the sentence (baked).* *Next, write this sentence:* "Cindy secretly baked cookies." *Ask students what was added—the word* secretly. *Explain that it is an adverb because it describes how the teacher baked the cookies. Ask the students to speculate why the teacher would secretly bake the cookies.* *Write this sentence:* "Cindy secretly and carefully baked cookies." *Call on a student to run to the board and touch the new adverb. Once again, give this student a cookie to eat as a reward.* *Next, write this sentence:* "Sly Cindy secretly and carefully baked cookies." *Ask students to identify the new word,* sly. *Explain that this new word describes the noun, Cindy, so it is an adjective.* *Ask students to point out the other noun in the sentence: cookies. Now say: "Well, we could have an adjective for that noun as well."*

	What and Why	How
		Next, write this sentence on the board:
		"Sly Cindy secretly and carefully baked bug cookies."
		Students will laugh because some students already ate a few cookies. Have a student identify the new adjective, and ask them if they want a cookie as a reward. The students will laugh.
		(This lesson can continue with direct object, indirect object, prepositions, or any other parts of speech that the students might be currently learning. And, it can be as gross—meaning as fun*—as you want to make it!)*
	Students talk about it or act it out.	*Students form teams of two. Each team makes a set of cards with each word from the sentence on a separate card. Teams work to sort the cards into categories: noun, adjective, adverb, and verb.*
Day 2	Make the concept real.	*Invite students to be engaged in the next sentence exercise. Write another three-word sentence on the board, similar to "Cindy baked cookies." For example, "Johnny built sandcastles." Ask students to identify the names of the words again, and then to act out the sentence. Develop the sentence just like it happened on Day 1, by adding one new word at a time. Each time, the students first identify what the new word is, then they act it out again. Be sure to include at least one word that is humorous in a gross way, such as "Johnny built booger sandcastles!"*
	Students practice in pairs or groups.	*Divide students into pairs, and have them make their own gross sentences on chart paper, with the requirement that each sentence must have at least one noun, adjective, adverb, and verb (or whatever grammar terms you are currently focusing on). Students must also write each component in a different color. For example: nouns in blue, verbs in red, adverbs in orange, and adjectives in purple.*
Day 3	Students retell the concept.	*Students present their gross sentences to the class. After each group presents, the class cheers and praises the group.*
Day 4	Show the students how to memorize the content.	*By now, students usually are close to knowing each part of the sentence they are learning because of the strong visuals used when writing out the sentence,*

(Continued)

What and Why		How
		and because they had such fun making it gross. Reinforce their memories by asking them to close their eyes and remember the sentences about the bug cookies. Ask these four questions:
		(1) Which person made them? (Noun.)
		(2) What was the action? (Verb.)
		(3) How did they make them? (Adverb.)
		(4) What kind of cookies? (Adjective.)
		In pairs, ask them to repeat this with the sentences they created yesterday, where one student asks these same questions, and the other answers. Then, they can reverse roles. Finally, each pair trades sentences with another pair, so they have new material to work on, and they repeat this process.
Day 5	Test day! Prove they are successful learners!	*Post 14 sentences in various places around the room. Tell students to choose 10 of these sentences and to write them down on a sheet of notebook paper with the nouns in blue, verbs in red, adverbs in orange, and adjectives in purple.*
	Celebrate!	*When the test scores are tabulated, make a graph celebrating their success. Play some fun—if possible, gross—songs while these graphs are being made, such as "Dead Skunk in the Middle of the Road" by Loudon Wainwright III.*

Adjustments for K–2: Teach using the same basic sequence, but focus solely only *nouns* (or *verbs*) with very simple sentences. During the activity on Day 1, rather than just having students point, ask them to *underline* the appropriate word with a designated color. Also, it's important to note that the sets of cards the students will use to sort the words into categories should be written out in advance.

If there is enough class time on Day 1, have students brainstorm vocabulary words they are learning that are nouns or verbs. For Day 2, prepare vocabulary cards for the kids to mix and match. If possible, use *their* names for nouns because they can read those. After working with a partner to sequence the cards in a sentence, the students could copy them on paper.

Green Light Strategies Used

- *Memory*—The different colors used when writing down the different parts of the sentences serve as a specific memory device.
- *Movement*—Walking up to get a cookie on the first day adds movement; acting out the sentences on the second day adds movement.
- *Novelty*—Students are always engaged by anything gross!
- *Tone*—The use of the four questions, repeated several times on Day 4, will help auditory learners better remember and distinguish the different parts of the sentences.
- *Emotions*—Again, using gross things will make them laugh and enjoy the lesson.
- *Socialization*—Students work in pairs many times throughout this lesson set.
- *Drama*—Students act out the sentences on Day 2.
- *Visuals*—Writing down the sentences they create, in different colors, will serve as a strong visual aspect of the lesson.

High-Five Principles Used

1. *True Learning Communities*—Creating their own gross sentences reinforces the essential content of the lesson, but it also allows students to take charge of one aspect of the process, which enhances their sense of ownership of, and thus their commitment to, the subject at hand.

3. *Teach to the Moment*—Students at the elementary level are inevitably intrigued by things that are weird or gross. This is truly fascinating within their world at this age, so a lesson set designed using anything along this line instantly has a better chance of success than one which uses dry, boring, uninteresting content as the base of the lesson.

4. *Learning Beyond Listening*—Students are deeply involved throughout this lesson set. The teacher is only ever "telling" when first introducing each part of a sentence. Other than those moments, students are learning by doing.

5. *The Learning Spiral*—Students are learning by adding only one word at a time, and the teacher does not add another word until all students are confident about the current list. Students celebrate at the end of the lesson set.

LESSON SET 8: WAYS WE ARE SMART

The red light method of teaching the concept of multiple intelligences is to present a matrix or grid explaining the various intelligences. The Green Light method involves personal connections, art, and drama.

Materials: construction paper, markers, colored pencils, the book *How We Are Smart* by W. Nikola-Lisa (2006), and printed pictures of celebrities and famous people

Subject: Multiple Intelligences

	What and Why	How
Day 1	Introduce the concept by getting students physically engaged with some funny movements and by telling them a story.	Say to your students, "How many of you know someone who is very talented in math? Raise your pinky in the air. How many know someone who is talented at building and creating things? Put your thumb on your nose. Everyone is talented in some way. Some are talented in a few ways, some in others. Everyone is smart in some unique way."
		Read How We Are Smart by W. Nikola-Lisa out loud to the class. This is a collection of poems. As you are reading, ask students to draw pictures of what they are hearing.
	Students talk about it or act it out.	Students share what they drew with a partner after the story. They then make some type of connection between themselves and one of the famous characters in the book. They do this by writing on a piece of paper:
		I am like _____ because I am _____.
		Now, they can draw a picture representing this connection.
Day 2	Make the concept real.	List the "Ways We Are Smart" on the board:
		Nature
		Number—math and logic
		Word—language and/or writing
		Music
		Picture—art
		Body—sports, kinesthetic
		People—interpersonal
		Self—intrapersonal
		Show pictures of celebrities, sports stars, and famous people. Ask students to call out which celebrities are smart in which ways. For example. Tiger Woods is body smart, Thomas Jefferson was word smart, Picasso was picture smart.

	What and Why	How
	Students practice in pairs or groups.	*Students take the short "In Which Ways Are You Smart?" questionnaire and tally up their scores. (See the High-Five Toolkit, p. 179).*
Day 3	Students retell the concept to show understanding.	*Independently, on construction paper, students draw a self-portrait that includes somehow showing the two or three top ways they are smart. They then decorate the picture with symbols for their type of intelligence. For example, if a student finds that he is music and people smart, then he might draw a self-portrait holding hands with someone while with music notes float around his head. Students share their pictures with other students, and they explain what they drew.*
Day 4	Show the students how to memorize the content.	*For each intelligence, make up a hand movement as a class. For example, for* self smart, *students might point to themselves; for* picture smart, *they might use their finger to draw an imaginary picture in the air.*
Day 5	Test day! Prove they are successful learners!	*This skill does not require a test. However, students can share their ways that they are smart with the class by getting into groups with others who have the same "smarts" as themselves and acting out the essence of that intelligence. For example, the* musical *bunch can each pretend to play a different instrument, saying, "We are music smart and we rock!"*
	Celebrate!	*After students share, display the self-portraits on the wall along with a "Ways We Are Smart" class graph, showing how many students are smart in each area.*

Adjustments for K–2: This strategy can be taught exactly as described. For the questionnaire, the teacher can read it aloud while the students tally.

Green Light Strategies Used

- *Memory*—The lesson uses an action for each way of being smart.
- *Connections*—Students see how famous people are smart in their particular areas of expertise.
- *Novelty*—Knowing that everyone—*everyone*—is smart will be intriguing to all kids, and they will start investigating in *what ways* their classmates are smart.

- *Tone*—The teacher reads the story aloud.
- *Emotions*—Students will become excited knowing they truly are smart, and they will want to share this with others.
- *Socialization*—Students are sharing with each other what they drew during the story, and they share their self-portraits.
- *Drama*—Students act out how they are smart in different groups, in the celebration phase of the lesson set.
- *Visuals*—The students create self-portraits that include their own personal symbols showing how they are smart.

High-Five Principles Used

2. *Optimum Learning Conditions*—Many students are amazed to discover they truly *are* smart. This sometimes shocking moment of discovery creates a sense of self-power and self-worth, which provides a powerful foundation for many future classroom activities. The self-confidence they feel will be the launching pad for taking risks and learning by walking boldly into the unknown, regardless of the subject matter.

3. *Teach to the Moment*—What's real for most young students is the sense that they truly are smart, clever, and intelligent—or *want* to be! The minute the teacher unleashes this idea, they latch onto it immediately, and they urgently want to investigate it further.

4. *Learning Beyond Listening*—Students are not merely listening to an explanation of the ways of being smart or merely listening to the stories from the book. They are actively involved in process of discovery as they make connections, draw pictures, and share their ideas, insights, and impressions.

LESSON SET 9: DOODLE-PREDICT

The red light method of teaching reading comprehension is for students to read stories and answer comprehension questions. The Green Light method involves drawing, music, and celebrating success (Jing, Yuan, & Liu, 1999, pp. 133–134).

Materials: the book *Thank You, Mr. Falker* by Patricia Polacco (1998); Doodle-Predict sheets (see the High-Five Toolkit, p. 180); pencils; colored pencils; print outs of pictures of weather satellites or clouds, rain, and so on; and a video clip of a weather forecaster

Subject: Making Predictions When Reading

	What and Why	How
Day 1	Introduce the concept with a discussion about something they are all familiar with.	Say to your students, "How many of you have ever watched a weather forecaster on TV? Do they know for 100% certain that the weather will be what they say?" (No!) "What do they use to predict the weather?" (Pictures!) Show several satellite pictures of weather. "Well, we are going to be weather forecasters today! We'll be looking at pictures to predict an outcome." Explain what predict means if students are not familiar with this concept.
	Students talk about it, or act it out.	Students sit in pairs or small groups. They look at various satellite weather photos and make weather predictions. Remind students they must be specific when saying their predictions; no pronouns or vague words are allowed. The viewers are counting on you!
Day 2	Make the concept real.	Show an actual clip of a weather forecaster. On an overhead projector (or drawn on the board), show the Doodle-Predict sheet. (As shown in the High-Five Toolkit.) Tell students this sheet will be the data sheet for the forecasters. Say to them, "Instead of watching satellite photos, we will read books and attempt to predict what will happen next. So, we are like 'Reading' Weather Scientists." Read the story Thank You, Mr. Falker to the class, stopping at various points for the students to doodle (draw what they just heard read to them) and to predict (write a complete sentence, using specific nouns, predicting what will happen next in the story). For example, read pages 1, 2, and stop at the end of page 3. Now, play soft music, and give the command, "Doodle!" This is the cue for students to draw a representation of what was just read. Next, read pages 4, 5, and stop at an exciting part of the story. Then say, "Predict!" This is the cue for students to write a thoughtful prediction in the next box marked PREDICT. Play the same soft music while they are writing their predictions.

(Continued)

(Continued)

	What and Why	How
	Students practice in pairs or groups.	*In pairs, students share their responses and retell the story. Encourage them to use this sentence: I predicted _____ because_____.*
Day 3	Students retell the concept.	*In pairs, students discuss what it means to make predictions and why this might be important when reading.*
Day 4	Show the students how to memorize the content.	*Repeat this idea with another story. Remind students that they will remember this story better because of the pictures they draw.*
Day 5	Test day! Prove they are successful learners!	*Let students select a story on their reading level. On a Doodle-Predict sheet, ask them to create appropriate pictures and thoughtful predictions. You could even have a miniconference with each student to help them better understand and assess the predictions.*
	Celebrate!	*Make a class display called "We Love to Doodle!" And, display everyone's doodle-predict sheets.*

Adjustments for K–2: You can still teach the strategies, but for the Predict part of the sheet, the students can either draw what they predict or pause to tell it to a partner. If pictures accompany the story, kindergarten students might also predict the weather based on visual and physical clues (for example, what the sky looks like or the clothes people are wearing).

Green Light Strategies Used

- *Memory*—Drawing on the Doodle-Predict sheets will go a long way toward helping students remember this idea.
- *Connections*—Starting the lesson set by making the connection to what weather forecasters do helps students understand the process better and see that people do use this idea for something very real.
- *Movement*—Students move as they gather around the teacher to hear the story, and they move again when they find a place to sit on the floor to draw. They will also move as they form groups to share their predictions.
- *Novelty*—The idea of making predictions, guessing, what is going to happen in a story will be unusual to many students, and it will keep them intrigued and engaged.

- *Tone*—The teacher telling the story is a different "tone" in the class-room. The use of specific music while they draw their predictions also creates a unique tone.
- *Emotions*—The excitement at guessing will keep students emotionally alert. When they predict correctly, they will feel successful (Egan & Judson, 2008, pp. 20–25).
- *Socialization*—Students are sharing their Doodle-Prediction pages.
- *Visuals*—The use of drawing in this lesson set will make the entire activity come alive for most students, and it will certainly make it memorable.

High-Five Principles Used

1. *True Learning Communities*—Celebrating by posting everyone's Doodle-Predict pages on the wall helps bring everyone together at the end of the lesson set. They see they are all working together, and some student's predictions will match other students', while everyone has something unique about his or her Doodle-Predict page.

2. *Optimum Learning Conditions*—Students are playing a much safer role in this activity than in a traditionally structured lesson. Instead of needing to find a right answer, they only need to make a guess as to what is going to happen. As one can never guess 100% right all the time, it is inherently OK for students to be "incorrect" when making predictions.

4. *Learning Beyond Listening*—The fact that the teacher has students actually *making* these predictions, not just thinking about them, is a critical distinction between the red and Green Light approaches to teaching. In addition, the fact that students are given time to draw their predictions means that a solid chunk of focused time will be spent on it, increasing the chances students will remember the idea.

LESSON SET 10: TRAINS AND TRANSITIONS

The red light method of teaching the use of transition words in writing sentences is to show examples and have students insert them into their own paragraphs. The Green Light method involves movement, conversation, practice, and interactive stories.

Materials: sentence strips with one-inch slits cut on one end, additional small paper strips cut into four-inch by one-inch lengths, markers, *Tim the Train* story handout and Transition Train poster (both shown below)

To prepare: Create 10 sentence sets consisting of two sentences that can be linked with a transition word. For example, a sentence set might contain the following two sentences: "I studied for my test," and, "I earned a good mark." These two sentences are a set because they could be linked with the transition words *therefore* or *consequently*. For each sentence set, on the small strips of paper, write down four or five possible transition words that might be used to join the sentences together. Include at least one correct choice (put a star on the back of the correct ones), and two or three incorrect choices. These smaller strips will actually be able to slide into the slits made on the sentence strips, linking the sentences.

Next, create the following example sentence set that will be used when the concept is first introduced, using the two sentences "I have a well-behaved class," and, "I enjoy teaching them." Write these on two strips of paper; then, on four of the small strips of paper, write the transition words *first, therefore, however,* and *finally.*

Subject: Sentence Transitions

	What and Why	How
Day 1	Introduce the concept with a story.	*Read the "Tim the Train" story without the transition words to the class. (See story on p. 158)*
		Ask students how they enjoyed the story. Ask if there seemed to be anything missing. Now, explain they are going to hear the story again, but this time something will be different.
		Read the story aloud again. This time, read the story with the transition words. Be sure to raise the tone of your voice when you say each of the transition words.
	Students talk about it or act it out.	*Ask the students which version of the story they liked better. They will usually agree that words like* consequently, therefore, *and* however *made the story more interesting.*
		Use this discussion to explain what linking, or transition, words are and how they are used in a story. Ask students to think of more transition words and share these with each other.
Day 2	Make the concept real.	*Remind students about Tim and how in the story he needed links to succeed. Explain that, when we are writing, we all need to use links, but we especially need to use the* correct *links to make our story truly come alive for the reader.*
		Explain that some of the transition words actually linked two sentences together. Demonstrate this by using the example sentence set. Show that in this

What and Why	How
	example the word therefore *is a great transition because it connects the sentences in a way that makes sense, and it also makes the idea more interesting. Show how the other transition words would not make sense if they were used.*
	Display the Transition Train poster (shown on p. 157), and explain that there are four main types of transitions.
	Then, help them remember the four different types of transitions by acting out each type:
	Time: *Students point to their wrist, as if they are pointing to a watch.*
	Relationships: *Students make both hands into a single fist and twirl their fisted hands in a circle, as if bringing people together.*
	Opposites: *Students push their arms out to the sides and up as if pushing two things apart.*
	Conclusion: *Students quickly bring their arms down to their hips as if completing an action.*
	In small groups, students practice each of these motions numerous times until they are certain they remember the action and the word for all four types of transition words.
Students practice in pairs or groups.	*Create stations around the room where students will practice the concept. At each station, place one sentence set, consisting of strips of paper with two sentences, and four or five smaller pieces of paper with transition word choices written on them.*
	Students now go to a station with their teams and decide which transition word would best link the two sentences. They can physically connect the two sentences by sliding the slip of paper with the proper transition word into the slits on the ends of the sentences. (They can see if they have chosen the right transition word by flipping it over; on the back of the correct one will be a small star.)
	When students have discovered the correct transition word at one station, they move to another station with a new set of sentences and work together to find the correction transition word for this station. In this way, they continue until they have visited all of the stations.

(Continued)

	What and Why	How
Day 3	Students retell the concept to show understanding.	*First, all students practice the physical actions for each of the four types of transition words. Next, students redo the station activity, but in different groups. This time, after they have chosen the correct transition word, they must decide which type of transition this one is, and they must do the action for that type. Finally, students explain to each other why this is the best transition word to join these two sentences together. They must agree on an explanation before moving to the next station.*
Day 4	Show the students how to memorize the content.	*As with Day 3, all students practice the physical actions for each of the four types of transition words. Now, read the "Tim the Train" story, with the transitions, one more time to the students. This time, students act out the type of transition word whenever they hear it. (Note: Students frequently like this activity. If they are enjoying it, repeat it several times to help reinforce the concept.)*
Day 5	Test day! Prove they are successful learners!	*Write five or six stories on poster paper and display them around the room. Leave numbered blanks where there is need for transition words. Students are given an answer sheet with corresponding numbered blanks. Each student individually picks three of the posted paragraphs. They then walk around the room and write the transition words on their answer sheet that they think are most appropriate for each space in the three paragraphs they have chosen.*
	Celebrate!	*Play train-themed music, such as "Love Train" by the O'Jays, "Morning Train" by Sheena Easton, or "The Locomotion" by Little Eva, and do a conga line around the classroom!*

Adjustments for K–2: This concept is actually often the *reverse* of what K–2 focuses on. Teachers of these students frequently spend enormous amounts of time "unhooking" the trains, because everything is written as one long sentence connected with *and*. However, the train analogy works perfectly well for teaching this idea.

When they are ready to learn the proper use of transitions, consider using basically the same approach; however, only teach these students the *time* aspect of transitions, using the words *first, next,* and *last.* For the assessment portion of the lesson set, instead of asking the students to make up their own transition words, provide them with two choices where they only need to circle the correct transition word.

Transition Train Poster

ALL ABOARD THE TRANSITION TRAIN

Type	Usage	Examples
TIME	Sequence of events	First, Second, Next, Suddenly, Meanwhile
RELATIONSHIPS	Two related thoughts about the same subject	Therefore, Consequently, Furthermore, Accordingly
OPPOSITES	Two opposing viewpoints connected	However, In contrast, On the other hand, On the contrary, Nevertheless
CONCLUSIONS	Ending	Finally, In conclusion, Thus, For this reason

Example

Correct: My dog does not like ham treats. *Therefore,* I gave him chicken.

Incorrect: My dog does not like ham treats. *Nevertheless,* I gave him chicken.

Remember, when using transition words, be sure to use them *correctly.* You might use several transition words in a single paragraph, but they are not needed in *every* sentence. Too many transitions can make the writing seem phony or forced.

TIM THE TRAIN

(The story without transition words)

Once, there was an old train named Tim. The train had problems. He was a loner. He did not work well with other train cars. _____, his days were harder and longer than any other train. Other trains had links to many cars to help them along. ----------------------------, Tim did not have any links to other cars. One day, something happened to change Tim's life as a train. ...., a car with links came by needing a job. Tim was not interested. _____, he ignored the car. ...., the car sat around while Tim laboriously traveled back and forth. ...., Tim's wheels started to squeal. He was working too hard. All of the years of working alone were getting to him. _ _ _ _ _ _ _ _ _ _, Tim hired the car and the links attached to it. ✱✱✱✱✱✱✱✱✱✱✱✱✱✱, the links and the car helped him move more smoothly on the train tracks. Tim learned the lesson that sometimes you need a little help from links to move you on your way smoothly.

TIM THE TRAIN

(The story with transition words)

Once, there was an old train named Tim. The train had problems. He was a loner. He did not work well with other train cars. **Therefore,** his days were harder and longer than any other train. Other trains had links to many cars to help them along. **However,** Tim did not have any links to other cars. One day, something happened to change Tim's life as a train. **First,** a car with links came by needing a job. Tim was not interested. **Accordingly,** he ignored the car. **Next,** the car sat around while Tim laboriously traveled back and forth. **Suddenly,** Tim's wheels started to squeal. He was working too hard. All of the years of working alone were getting to him. **Finally,** Tim hired the car and the links attached to it. **Consequently,** the links and the car helped him move more smoothly on the train tracks. Tim learned the lesson that sometimes you need a little help from links to move you on your way smoothly.

8 The High-Five Toolkit

ATTITUDE IS A LITTLE THING THAT MAKES A BIG DIFFERENCE

The Memory Pegs	Editing Doctor Practice Essays
The Spelling Hopscotch Grid	In Which Ways Are You Smart?
The Math 100-Square Grid	Doodle-Predict Sheet

THE MEMORY PEGS

Below are the memory pegs introduced under Day 1 in the Five-by-Five chapter.

The Peg	The Action
1. Sun	Make a circle with your hands.
2. Eyes	Bring two fingers to your eyes.
3. Triangle	Draw a triangle in the air with your fingers.
4. Stove	Touch all four burners on a stove.
5. Fingers	Hold up the five fingers of one hand.
6. Sticks	Pick up sticks from the ground.
7. 7 Up	Take a big drink from a can of 7-Up.
8. Octopus	Put your arms out like an octopus.
9. Line	Draw a line in the air in front of you.
10. Hen	Flap your arms like a chicken's wings.
11. Fence	Put two fingers in the air, and make a series of fence posts.
12. Eggs	Crack an imaginary egg.
13. Black Cat	Pet the cat.
14. Heart	Make a heart in the air in front of you with your fingers.
15. Fame	Spread Your arms wide, and say, "Fame!"
16. Driving	Drive an imaginary car.
17. Magazine	Turn the pages of an imaginary magazine.
18. Vote	Make a check mark in the air.
19. TV Remote	Click the imaginary remote at the imaginary TV.
20. 20–20 Vision	Make circles with your hands around your eyes.

Here's how you can use them:

Step One: Learning the Pegs *Yourself!*

First, before you can share this with your students, you'll need to know how to use the pegs yourself. Learn them by first saying the number, then saying the peg associated with that number while doing the motion. For example, to learn the first peg, out loud say, "One, sun." At the same time, do the action of making a circle with your hands in the air in front of you. Next, say, "Two, eyes." At the same time, do the action of bringing two fingers towards your eyes, pointing at them. Continue in this way until you feel confident you've learned all 20 of the pegs.

To verify that you really can remember them, try several things. First, give a friend the list of the 20 pegs to test you while you go through them in order. Remember, *always say the number, and then say the name of the peg as you do the action.* Next, try doing the 20 pegs backwards, starting at 20, and going down to 1. Again, ask your friend to make sure you get them all correct. Finally, ask your friend to call out random numbers between 1 and 20, and you tell them the peg while doing the action.

When you are confident you know the 20 pegs, you're ready for the next step . . .

Step Two: Using the Pegs Yourself

Here's how to use the pegs at a very basic level. Begin by making a random list of *20 common household* objects. We've filled in the first few, just to get you started, so please fill in the rest of the list. *Be sure to do this before you read on!*

1. book	11.
2. refrigerator	12.
3. lamp	13.
4.	14.
5.	15.
6.	16.
7.	17.
8.	18.
9.	19.
10.	20.

Now, suppose you wanted to memorize this list you've just created. How can you use the pegs to do it? To explain, it helps to know why they are referred to as pegs.

Have you ever seen pegs on the kitchen wall, where people hang various sets of keys? The words you've learned, connected to each number, can be used like mental pegs. You can "hang" a picture of the thing you want to remember onto the picture that's already in your head at each number. Here's how it works.

Take the first thing on this list you want to remember. How do you remember it's a book? You start by thinking of the peg you've learned for number one. Remember? It's the sun, and the motion is making a circle in front of you like a sun. The key is to *take the motion you already know—making a circle—start making it again, but then let it change into a motion that might remind you of a book.*

For example, you might start making the circle, then you square it off, and you say the word *book.* Starting the motion you already learned becomes the trigger for the motion, which changes into a specific motion that triggers the memory. Try it right now, do it in the air in front of you—start making a circle, and then change it into a square and say, "One, book." Remember, it's important to keep saying the number!

Let's try another one. The second entry on this list is a refrigerator. First, start making the motion for the second peg. Remember, the second peg is eyes, and the motion is your two fingers coming toward your eyes. Now, start that motion, but change it into something that will trigger a memory of a refrigerator. It could be anything that *you* want to make up, but for now, let's imagine that your fingers start coming towards your eyes, and then you bend them into hooks, which you use to open the refrigerator door, as you say, "Two, Refrigerator." Try that right now. Do it several times.

For the third entry, use the same idea: Start with the action you know for that peg, and change it into something that will trigger a memory of the item on the list. Can you make one up right now, before you read on? *Try it!* Perhaps, since the third peg is a triangle, and the motion is to make a triangle with your fingers, you could start making the triangle, but as your fingers come down, pull on an imaginary lamp cord, and say, "Three, lamp."

Now, continue memorizing the list you created, using this approach. For each item, start the motion of the peg you already know, and then change it to become a motion that triggers the memory of the item on the list. Do this for each one several times, always saying the number and the item as you do the motion. Continue down the list until you've done all 20. Finally, grab a sheet of paper and write down the 20 things on that list!

If you're like most people, you'll get most of them (perhaps all of them) right away! It's OK to celebrate—this is great! Yet, while this instant success tends to startle many people who are trying it for the first time, it's really not magic; it's just using the basic way our memory works naturally.

To make sure you have the hang of using the memory pegs, you might want to repeat this process several times, each time using a new list, before you introduce it to your students. Only do it once a day, at most. When you're confident you understand how the process works, you're ready for the next step . . .

Step Three: Demonstrating the Pegs to Your Students

Here's one way to introduce your students to the pegs. Done properly, it's completely amazing to the students and enjoyable to do! It's mentioned briefly under Day 1 in the Five-by-Five chapter; however, we'll expand on it here.

First, ask your students to call out 20 household items, and get a couple of volunteers to write them on the board. Don't tell them why you're doing it; just ask them to give suggestions while you or your volunteers write them up. When you have 20 things written on the board, tell the students you'll come back to these later, and get them busy doing some type of activity where they are working with each other. When they're busy, use the peg strategy to memorize the pegs. Don't be too obvious about your hand motions, and take as much time as you need.

When you feel you have the list memorized, you can start. Tell your students you're going to memorize the list. Ask them to time 20 seconds for you. When they say, "Go!," turn your back on them and look at the 20 things on the board. Use this time to check once again that you *do* know them! Then, turn around, and without looking at the board, start saying the items in order. They'll be staring at you, amazed! And then, if you're feeling confident, ask them to call out random numbers, such as 7 or 15, and show that you can remember any of the items from the list, even when they are called out at random. And of course—celebrate!

Now that you've amazed them, you're ready for the next step . . .

Step Four: Teaching the Pegs to the Students

Teaching the pegs to the students follows the same sequence that you used when you were learning them yourself:

1. Explain that, for them to do this, first they have to learn some pegs. Make it clear why they are called pegs, using the explanation from this section.

2. Teach the students the 20 pegs, going in order and asking them to repeat each one, always doing the actions.

3. Next, students practice the pegs in pairs or trios, doing them first in order, then backwards, then testing each other with random peg numbers.

4. When they all know the pegs, celebrate!

5. Demonstrate how you used the motion of each peg to make a connection to the list of items on the board. Do the first few with them, and then get them to work together to memorize the rest of the list. Give them five minutes at most!

6. After the five minutes are over, erase the items from the board! Ask your students to work together to write down the 20 items from the board. Celebrate their success!

It's OK to now tell the students the truth: You actually took a bit more time to learn the pegs while they were involved in the activity. You certainly don't have to, if you want to maintain an air of mystery and magic! However, many teachers—following the idea of *Tell Students Everything*—will want to talk about it, explaining they did it to create a state of amazement, which helps students get excited about learning. And they should be excited even if it takes a few minutes instead of 20 seconds; in many ways, that's *still very magical!*

When students have proven to themselves they can memorize 20 individual items this way, you're ready for the final step.

Step Five: Using the Pegs to Learn Content

The final piece in teaching the memory pegs is to show students how to use them to remember important information. Interestingly, once the basic idea is in place, this last part is surprisingly simple yet incredibly powerful.

The key is to isolate the important points from any unit or lesson. Write these points on the board. For example, if your students are doing a history unit, on the day before the test, write up the 20 most important facts, such as names, dates, or locations. Give students time to work together and use the pegs to memorize them. When students can remember these keys points, they'll easily be able to recall other information *related* to these central points.

Can students remember multiple lists? Yes, they can! Meaning, the pegs can be used to remember key points from several different content areas if necessary. Try them in various ways with various subject areas, and watch how flexible, adaptable, and *useful* these memory pegs can be.

THE SPELLING HOPSCOTCH GRID

Figure 8.1 is the diagram of the Spelling Hopscotch Grid mentioned in Principle 4 and Day 1 of the Five-by-Five chapter. You can make this grid in a variety of ways, using electrical tape, masking tape, a tarp with the letters on it, laminated squares of paper adhered to the floor, or even drawn directly on the classroom floor using permanent markers. Each box is approximately 12 inches square.

Figure 8.1 The Spelling Hopscotch Grid

	P		Q	
T	A	R	U	B
	C	O	Y	
D	S	F	E	I
	N	T	G	
X	I	L	H	J
	K	E	S	
A	R	O	M	V
	W	N	U	
		Z		

Students use this grid to learn their spelling words. Here is how to conduct a spelling lesson using the Spelling Grid:

To begin, all students stand in a loose circle around the Spelling Grid. Select one student, and give him a list of your spelling words. The selected student picks a word that everyone will work together to learn, and announces the word in a loud voice. All students echo back the word, saying it loudly and clearly.

The student then calls out the first letter of the selected word. All students echo back the letter aloud *and point to it on the grid* while the student holding the sheet of paper jumps onto that letter on the Spelling Grid. Then, the student calls out the second letter of the word, the students again echo back the second letter and point to it, while the student on the grid hops onto it. Continue this process until the entire word has been spelled—at which point all students celebrate.

Choose a strong physical method of celebration. For example, all students could push the palms of their hands toward the ceiling, and—if the name of the student was 'Brandon'—say, "Go Brandon! Go Brandon! Go Brandon!"

An important detail: When learning a capitalized word, be sure the students call out not just the letter but actually say, "*Capital* E!" This serves as a constant reminder that the word is capitalized.

This is the basic format for using the grid to learn spelling words. However, like many of the ideas included in this book, it can be adjusted or tweaked in a variety of ways. When making changes, however, keep in mind an important distinction: When the Spelling Grid is used as described here, students are using *all three primary learning modalities:*

- **Visual:** All students are learning through *sight* when looking for and pointing to the next letter the student on the grid will jump to.
- **Auditory:** All students are learning through *sound* when listening to the selected student call out the word, when listening to the student call out the next letter, and when calling out the word and letter themselves.
- **Kinesthetic:** All students are learning through *movement*. While the selected student actually on the grid is getting the kinesthetic benefit of learning by jumping on the letters, all students are actually learning by watching the movement. This is a combination visual-movement mechanism that significantly aids overall recall, meaning that, when they need to spell the word, they can close their eyes and remember *seeing* the other student jumping onto each letter and thus remember how to spell the word. They are also staying kinesthetically engaged by celebrating at the end of each word.

This distinction is important to remember when making adjustments to the basic idea of using the Spelling Grid. Whatever changes are made, ask yourself if all three primary learning modalities are being given an avenue of expression from which all students can learn?

K–2 Adjustment: At the younger levels, students may need to start with a simpler task and even a smaller size grid! Therefore, here's a possible variation[4]. Start with a simpler pattern, such as the one shown in Figure 8.2, with eight squares.

Much like the Spelling Grid, you could make this pattern using masking tape on the floor of the classroom, on a tarp, or even on a regular white cloth sheet. Next, make cards with the letters of the alphabet on them—one side has lowercase letters, and the reverse has the uppercase version of the same letter, such as *a* on one side and *A* on the other.

Place the letter cards on the corner of each square (see Figure 8.3). Ask students to hop from one end to the other, saying either the name or the sound of the letter, depending on their current stage of development.

This approach has several advantages for younger students:

- It focuses on what they are learning at that time, which is simply the letters or the sounds of the letters.
- It is short, so many students can be involved in a short amount of time.
- It is flexible, with the letter cards being changed anytime: after a few students have taken a turn, from day to day, or week to week.
- It is also flexible in that one day students could be learning lower-cases letters, and the next day they might be learning upper-case letters.
- The idea of simply hopping from one end to the other gives students a clear focus.

As another option, you could replace the letter cards with small beanbags with letters sewn on either side. This has the added advantage of being something fun to touch and hold, which might better engage students of this age.

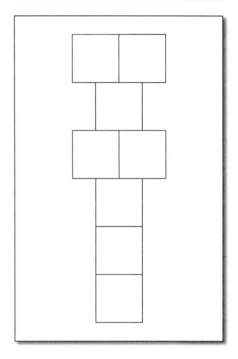

Figure 8.2 K–2 Hopscotch Grid

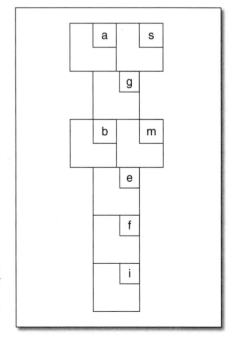

Figure 8.3 K–2 Hopscotch Grid With Letters

THE MATH 100-SQUARE GRID

Figure 8.4 is the diagram of the Math 100-Square Grid, as previously mentioned in both Principle 4 and Day 1 of the Five-by-Five chapter.

Figure 8.4   Math 100-Square Grid

1	2	3	4	5	6	7	8	9	10
11	12	13	14	15	16	17	18	19	20
21	22	23	24	25	26	27	28	29	30
31	32	33	34	35	36	37	38	39	40
41	42	43	44	45	46	47	48	49	50
51	52	53	54	55	56	57	58	59	60
61	62	63	64	65	66	67	68	69	70
71	72	73	74	75	76	77	78	79	80
81	82	83	84	85	86	87	88	89	90
91	92	93	94	95	96	97	98	99	100

You can teach a variety of mathematical concepts using this pattern, depending on the skill levels of your students and what concepts they are learning. Here are some ideas for just a few of the many things you could use it for.

- **Counting:** (Younger students) Invite a student to "march" up the numbers, and ask everyone to count out loud. Then, go backwards. Or, count by twos by having a student jump up by twos (or threes) while the class counts along with the person jumping.
- **Odds and Evens:** (Younger students) Ask all students to run and stand on an even number. Next, ask them to switch to standing on an odd number. Or, ask all girls to stand on even numbers and the boys on odd numbers. Then, they switch. Or, ask one student to run and stand on a number, and the class decides if they are on an even or odd number.
- **Basic Math:** Invite all students to stand on any number. Once they are all standing on one, ask them to add 5, and stand on the answer. Or, ask them to subtract 3, and stand on the answer. Or, ask them to multiply by 2, and stand on the answer. This works with any variation or combination of adding, subtracting, or multiplying.
- **Musical Numbers, Basic Math:** Music plays while all students are walking every which way on the grid. When the music stops, the teacher might say, "Odd!" and all students stand on an odd number. Then, more music plays, and when it stops, the teacher might say, "Even!" and all students must stand on an even number. Or, the teacher might say, "Any number larger than 31!" or, "Any number smaller than 40!"
- **Musical Numbers, Divisibility Rules:** The teacher might say, "Stand on any number that is divisible by two!" or, "Stand on any number divisible by three!" The key here is that most students will immediately start to race over to stand on a lower number, since those are the first ones that come to mind. However, if there are 28 students in a class, most students will have to start thinking of *higher* numbers. This helps them start working with larger numbers. There's also fun and laughter because they all *know* they all wanted to stand on the easy numbers, but those squares are quickly taken. To find a place to stand, they will have to use their divisibility rules—and they're allowed to help each other!
- **Twister:** This math-movement game combines some of the ideas already mentioned. Perhaps students are first asked to put their right foot on an odd number then their left foot on a number that is divisible by 5. When everyone has their balance, they could be asked

to put their left hand on an even number and right hand on a number divisible by 3!

- **Composites and Factors:** Students learn by working with a partner in the following way: First, music plays while all students wander on the math grid. When the music stops, one student stands on a two-digit number. It must be a composite number, meaning a number that can be factored. The other student sees what her partner is standing on and must then stand on any of the factors of that number. For example, if the first student chose to stand on the number 51, the second student could stand on either 3 or 17.

- **Mystery Numbers:** The teacher writes the numbers 1 through 100 on index cards, one number per card. The cards are shuffled, and each student picks a card but is not allowed to look at it. The students then hold their card up to their foreheads, where other students can see the number, but they can't see their own. The object of the game is for the students to figure out what number they have on their own foreheads.

  They do this by asking *other students* questions that have yes or no answers. For example, a student might ask another student, "Am I a composite number?" or, "Am I prime?" or, "Am I divisible by five?" Once they have an answer to work with, they can stand on a number and ask another student, "Am I this number?" If the answer is no, they ask another question, such as, "Am I divisible by three?" By repeatedly asking yes or no questions and then standing on a number and asking if they are on the right number, all students eventually discover the number they are holding on their forehead.

- **Table Dancing:** Two students face off on opposites sides of the square. The teacher calls out a multiplication problem, such as "Eight times seven." Students race each other to see who can stand on the answer first. Whoever wins gets 10 seconds to celebrate by dancing on the Math Table. Then, another pair of students goes, and then another.

- **Fact Families:** Students learn about math "fact families" the following way: The song "We Are Family" by Sly and the Family Stone is playing while students get in groups of three. When the music stops, they must work together to stand on any fact family, a group of three numbers where two numbers multiplied together equal the third number. Examples of fact families might be 4, 6, and 24, or 3, 7, and 21. When the song is played again, they must stand on a new fact family, such as 7, 5, and 35. So, if one runs and stands on the number 5, and another one is standing on the number 35, they have to work together to figure out that the third student must be standing on the number 7.

The key element in this game is to remember that *many students are playing!* Therefore, when the music stops, as they are working to find a fact family, someone might already be standing on a number the group needs, so they have to work together to find *another* fact family. This forces students to work with fact families they haven't noticed with before and larger numbers as well.

- **Fact Trees:** A "fact tree" consists of all the *prime factors* of a number. For example, the fact tree for the number 12 is 2, 2, and 3—because the prime numbers $2 \times 2 \times 3 = 12$. Or, the fact tree for the number 90 is 2, 3, 3, and 5 because the prime numbers $2 \times 3 \times 3 \times 5 = 90$.

  To learn fact trees, students are first organized in groups of three or four. The teacher selects one group and asks one of the group members to stand on a number, such as 21. The rest of the students in that group must now work together to figure out and stand on the fact tree for that number. In this case, the fact tree would consist simply of 3 and 7. When one group has created a fact tree, another group gets a turn, with a new starting number.

  However, what if the starting number was 36? First, the rest of the students in that group would work together to figure out and stand on the fact tree for that number. In this case, the fact tree would consist of 2, 2, 3, and 3. If a number is used more than once, such as two 2s, students must figure out how to have two of them standing in that small square!

  One of the keys to this activity is that, in making a fact tree, students will often accidentally stand on a number that is *not* prime. For example, when creating the fact tree for the number 12, one student in the group might stand on the number 2, while another one starts to stand on the number 6. But, as a fact tree contains only the *prime* factors, this is not a correct fact tree member, so other students are allowed to call out, "Find only primes! Find only primes!" This alerts the group that one of their numbers is not prime, and it allows them to adjust and find the correct fact tree. In this way, while primarily learning about fact trees, all students are also learning and reinforcing their knowledge of prime numbers.

Remember these examples are just a few of the almost endless variety of learning exercises you could create using this pattern on the floor. Let your imagination go, and see how else you might use it!

EDITING DOCTORS PRACTICE ESSAYS

As mentioned in Lesson 1, these are sample practice essays that can be used when first teaching students about the six key ideas to look for when editing their papers. Each essay contains one specific "illness." In addition, each essay is an example of a *different type of writing*.

Sick Essay 1

I Don't Want Your Germs!

Have you ever had a friend or family member get sick and then give the sickness to you? Who's job is it to make sure we don't get sick? It is our job. Too many people are careless about the spread of germs. I believe that schools should require students to sanitize there hands three times a day. They should do this because it is keeps germs from spreading, and students would not miss as much school from being sick.

Squirt, squirt! That's all it takes to defend yourself against germs. All students have to do is squirt on some hand sanitizer at the beginning of the day, at lunch, and at the end of the day. Teachers often request hand sanitizer for supplies. We need to start using them like we could of before. Germs need to be defeated.

Achoo! That is the sound of someone sneezing. When they sneeze, they get germs all over their hands. If they go to open a door or use a pencil, they can spread their germs. The hand sanitizer would make sure that the germs are killed before being spread. This can lead to fewer absences.

Its simple.

How many times do you stay home sick in a year? When you stay home from school you miss important information. We could have more students with prefect attendance if they didn't have to stay home with a cold. Hand sanitizer would pervent those colds.

If principles were smart, they would take my advice and make it a schoolwide rule to sanitize. It can only benfit the students.

- This is an example of a *persuasive* essay.
- The hidden illness is *spelling*.

The corrections are . . .

I Don't Want Your Germs!

Have you ever had a friend or family member get sick and then give the sickness to you? Whose job is it to make sure we don't get sick? It is our job. Too many people are careless about the spread of germs. I believe that schools should require students to sanitize their hands three times a day. They should do this because it is keeps germs from spreading, and students would not miss as much school from being sick.

Squirt, squirt! That's all it takes to defend yourself against germs. All students have to do is squirt on some hand sanitizer at the beginning of the day, at lunch, and at the end of the day. Teachers often request hand sanitizer for supplies. We need to start using them like we could have before. Germs need to be defeated.

Achoo! That is the sound of someone sneezing. When they sneeze, they get germs all over their hands. If they go to open a door or use a pencil, they can spread their germs. The hand sanitizer would make sure that the germs are killed before being spread. This can lead to fewer absences.

It's simple.

How many times do you stay home sick in a year? When you stay home from school, you miss important information. We could have more students with perfect attendance if they didn't have to stay home with a cold. Hand sanitizer would prevent those colds.

If principals were smart, they would take my advice and make it a schoolwide rule to sanitize. It can only benefit the students.

Sick Essay 2

sick as a Dog

Have you ever had surgery? I have. one time I had to get my tonsils taken out. It was not my idea of fun, and my dog had surgery on his paw the same day! My dog and I really bonded during that time.

It was a foggy morning. I had to wake up extra early to get to the hospital for my tonsillectomy. That's a fancy way of saying tonsil surgery. I wasn't allowed to eat any breakfast because that is one of the rules of surgery: no food for 12 hours before. My dog, Rufus, was also getting surgery on his paw, and he had the same rule. My stomach was a sea of writhing snakes. My heart was pounding like a drum. I never had surgery before, so I was quite scared. I paced my room waiting for the time to leave. "We better get going now," bellowed my mom.

"I'll be right there, Mom," I shouted. When I got down stairs, my dad gave me a pat on the head.

"You okay, kiddo?" He asked.

"I'll be fine," I lied.

I gave Rufus a gigantic hug. Somehow, he seemed to hug me back to let me know that he could feel my nervousness. "You'll do just fine ol' boy," I assured him. "We'll heal together; I promise."

The surgery wasn't too bad. It just seemed like I took a big nap. When I got home, my parents gave me a lot of attention and ice cream. Rufus was already home when I came in. We just lay in my bed together, enjoying the way everyone was taking care of us.

getting tonsil surgery turned out to be an easy experience, and I know that Rufus felt better knowing that I was with him through his healing time. He liked it even better when I snuck him some of my ice cream. We'll never forget the time when we were both sick as a dog.

- This is an example of a *personal narrative* essay.
- The hidden illness is *capitalization.*

The corrections are . . .

Sick as a Dog

Have you ever had surgery? I have. One time I had to get my tonsils taken out. It was not my idea of fun, and my dog had surgery on his paw the same day! My dog and I really bonded during that time.

It was a foggy morning. I had to wake up extra early to get to the hospital for my tonsillectomy. That's a fancy way of saying tonsil surgery. I wasn't allowed to eat any breakfast because that is one of the rules of surgery: no food for 12 hours before. My dog, Rufus, was also getting surgery on his paw, and he had the same rule. My stomach was a sea of writhing snakes. My heart was pounding like a drum. I never had surgery before, so I was quite scared. I paced my room waiting for the time to leave. "We better get going now," bellowed my mom.

"I'll be right there, Mom," I shouted. When I got down stairs, my dad gave me a pat on the head.

"You okay, kiddo?" he asked.

"I'll be fine," I lied.

I gave Rufus a gigantic hug. Somehow, he seemed to hug me back to let me know that he could feel my nervousness. "You'll do just fine ol' boy," I assured him. "We'll heal together; I promise."

The surgery wasn't too bad. It just seemed like I took a big nap. When I got home, my parents gave me a lot of attention and ice cream. Rufus was already home when I came in. We just lay in my bed together, enjoying the way everyone was taking care of us.

Getting tonsil surgery turned out to be an easy experience, and I know that Rufus felt better knowing that I was with him through his healing time. He liked it even better when I snuck him some of my ice cream. We'll never forget the time when we were both sick as a dog.

Sick Essay 3

Broken Bone Blues

Crack! It hurts to break a bone! It's different for everyone, but the pain is often like the deep ache you get from a super bad stomach ache or headache. Some people may experience sharper pain, especially with an open fracture if the fracture is small, a kid may not feel much pain at all. Sometimes, a kid won't even be able to tell that he or she broke a bone! Broken bones can be a shock to the body, so here are some facts about what to do if you or someone you know breaks a bone.

Breaking a bone is a big shock to your whole body it's normal for you to receive strong messages from parts of your body that aren't anywhere close to the fracture. You may feel dizzy, woozy, or chilly from the shock. A lot of people cry for a while. Some people pass out until their bodies have time to adjust to all the signals they're getting. And, other people don't feel any pain right away because of the shock of the injury.

"Ouch, help me!" If you think you or someone else has broken a bone, the most important things to do are to stay calm, make sure the person is comfortable, tell an adult, or call 911. You should get help as soon as possible. There are some things that you should never do as well.

The worst thing for a broken bone is to move it this will hurt the person, and it can make the injury worse! In the case of a broken arm or leg, a grown up may be able to cushion or support the surrounding area with towels or pillows.

Broken bones are a fact of life. They do happen, but you can be prepared to minimize the pain. One super-important tip: If you're not sure what bone is broken or you think the neck or back is broken, do not try to move the injured person. Wait until a trained medical professional has arrived!

- This is an example of an *informational* essay.
- The hidden illness is *run-ons*.

The corrections are . . .

Broken Bone Blues

Crack! It hurts to break a bone! It's different for everyone, but the pain is often like the deep ache you get from a super bad stomach ache or headache. Some people may experience sharper pain, especially with an open fracture. If the fracture is small, a kid may not feel much pain at all. Sometimes, a kid won't even be able to tell that he or she broke a bone! Broken bones can be a shock to the body, so here are some facts about what to do if you or someone you know breaks a bone.

Breaking a bone is a big shock to your whole body. It's normal for you to receive strong messages from parts of your body that aren't anywhere close to the fracture. You may feel dizzy, woozy, or chilly from the shock. A lot of people cry for a while. Some people pass out until their bodies have time to adjust to all the signals they're getting. And, other people don't feel any pain right away because of the shock of the injury.

"Ouch, help me!" If you think you or someone else has broken a bone, the most important things to do are to stay calm, make sure the person is comfortable, tell an adult, or call 911. You should get help as soon as possible. There are some things that you should never do as well.

The worst thing for a broken bone is to move it. This will hurt the person, and it can make the injury worse! In the case of a broken arm or leg, a grown up may be able to cushion or support the surrounding area with towels or pillows.

Broken bones are a fact of life. They do happen, but you can be prepared to minimize the pain. One super-important tip: If you're not sure what bone is broken or you think the neck or back is broken, do not try to move the injured person. Wait until a trained medical professional has arrived!

Sick Essay 4

My Bed, My Haven

Thump! My head hits the pillow as I fall into a blissful sleep. My bed is my haven when I am sick or tired. It makes me feel safe, comfortable, and sleepy.

Do you feel safe in your bed? When I am in my bed, I feel like nothing can go wrong the comforter hugs me and tells me that everything will be all right the pillows brush my awful, pounding headaches away when I am sick. My bed is an island of safety and warmth.

I can just feel the silky soft smoothness of the sheets. They comfort me and make the troubles of the day disappear. My bed is the most comfortable place in my house. When I lay down, I lose myself in its softness.

"Good night!" It is always a good night in my bed. Sleeping is a breeze in my haven. Even when I am sick, my bed easily takes me off to dreamland. My bed makes dreams possible. Do you have a place in your house that makes you feel safe, comfortable, and sleepy? For me, it will be my beautiful bed.

- This is an example of a *personal narrative/descriptive* essay.
- The hidden illness is *indentitus.*

The corrections are . . .

My Bed, My Haven

Thump! My head hits the pillow as I fall into a blissful sleep. My bed is my haven when I am sick or tired. It makes me feel safe, comfortable, and sleepy.

Do you feel safe in your bed? When I am in my bed, I feel like nothing can go wrong. The comforter hugs me and tells me that everything will be all right. The pillows brush my awful, pounding headaches away when I am sick. My bed is an island of safety and warmth.

→I can just feel the silky soft smoothness of the sheets. They comfort me and make the troubles of the day disappear. My bed is the most comfortable place in my house. When I lay down, I lose myself in its softness.

"Good night!" It is always a good night in my bed. Sleeping is a breeze in my haven. Even when I am sick, my bed easily takes me off to dreamland. My bed makes dreams possible.

→Do you have a place in your house that makes you feel safe, comfortable, and sleepy? For me, it's my beautiful bed.

Sick Essay 5

Pesky Colds

Have you ever had a cold. Most Americans experience many colds in their lifetime. Colds occur during certain seasons, can be affected by the weather, and there are ways to prevent colds.

In the United States, most colds, occur during the fall, and winter. Beginning in late August or early September, the incidence of colds increases slowly for a few weeks and remains high until March or April, when it declines. The seasonal variation may relate to the opening of schools and to cold weather, which prompt people to spend more time indoors and increase the chances that viruses will spread from person to person?

Seasonal changes in relative humidity also may affect how often you get colds. The most common cold-causing viruses survive better when humidity is low during the colder months of the year. Cold weather also may make the nasal passages' lining drier and more vulnerable to viral infection.

Hand washing is the simplest and most effective way to keep from getting rhinovirus colds. Not, touching the nose or eyes is another. Individuals with colds should always sneeze or cough into a facial tissue, and promptly throw it away. If possible, one should avoid close, prolonged exposure to persons who have colds.

Most Americans get colds, but there are ways to understand and prevent them.

- This is an example of an *informational* essay.
- The hidden illness is *punctuation*.

The corrections are . . .

Pesky Colds

Have you ever had a cold? Most Americans experience many colds in their lifetime. Colds occur during certain seasons, can be affected by the weather, and there are ways to prevent colds.

In the United States, most colds_ occur during the fall_ and winter. Beginning in late August or early September, the incidence of colds increases slowly for a few weeks and remains high until March or April, when it declines. The seasonal variation may relate to the opening of schools and to cold weather, which prompt people to spend more time indoors and increase the chances that viruses will spread from person to person.

Seasonal changes in relative humidity also may affect how often you get colds. The most common cold-causing viruses survive better when humidity is low during the colder months of the year. Cold weather also may make the nasal passages' lining drier and more vulnerable to viral infection.

Hand washing is the simplest and most effective way to keep from getting rhinovirus colds. Not_ touching the nose or eyes is another. Individuals with colds should always sneeze or cough into a facial tissue, and promptly throw it away. If possible, one should avoid close, prolonged exposure to persons who have colds.

Most Americans get colds, but there are ways to understand and prevent them.

Sick Essay 6

Doug, the Dog Doctor

Woof, woof! That's what most people hearing when a dog barks, but not Doctor Doug. From the time he was little, he could talk to animals. He understood them, and they understood him. He always knew that he had to keep this talent a secret because most people did not believe that humans could understand dogs unless they were crazy. One time, he almost lost his job because someone caught him talking to his animal patients.

It is a cold morning in Ferretville. Doctor Doug was on his way to work. He was a vet in this town. Suddenly, the clouds swooped in and the day got drearier. Doctor Doug could sense that something bad was going to happen.

He will waves hello to Mr. Snoops. Mr. Snoops was a bitter old man who owned the barber shop across the street. He was jealous of all of the business Doctor Doug had and of his success. Mr. Snoops thought to himself, "There has to be a reason why so many animals want to be treated by Doctor Doug, and I am going to find out!"

"Why this is a nice surprise!" Doctor Doug crooned when Mr. Snoops walked into the animal clinic. "What can I do for you?" he asked with a smile.

"Oh, I just wanted to see how things were going," replied Mr. Snoops as he secretly hid a recording device under the examination table. He quickly left.

Doctor Doug talked to his animal patients all day as usual. When Mr. Snoops secretly took the recorder back and listened to it, he jumped for joy. "I finally got him!" he exclaimed.

The next day, the sun was shining, and the birds were singing their songs. This time when he will arrives to work, Doctor Doug saw men in white coats taking Mr. Snoops away.

"What's going on?" Doctor Doug asked one of the men.

"This guy went to the police with a tape of animal noises claiming he knows someone who talks to animals. We think we need to send him away to be evaluated. Sometimes, these old people come up with crazy ideas. Hopefully, he'll be back before you know it," he replied.

- This is an example of a *narrative* essay.
- The hidden illness is *tense*.

The corrections are . . .

Doug, the Dog Doctor

Woof, woof! That's what most people hear when a dog barks, but not Doctor Doug. From the time he was little, he could talk to animals. He understood them, and they understood him. He always knew that he had to keep this talent a secret because most people did not believe that humans could understand dogs unless they were crazy. One time, he almost lost his job because someone caught him talking to his animal patients.

It was a cold morning in Ferretville. Doctor Doug was on his way to work. He was a vet in this town. Suddenly, the clouds swooped in and the day got drearier. Doctor Doug could sense that something bad was going to happen.

He waved hello to Mr. Snoops. Mr. Snoops was a bitter old man who owned the barber shop across the street. He was jealous of all of the business Doctor Doug had and of his success. Mr. Snoops thought to himself, "There has to be a reason why so many animals want to be treated by Doctor Doug, and I am going to find out!"

"Why this is a nice surprise!" Doctor Doug crooned when Mr. Snoops walked into the animal clinic. "What can I do for you?" he asked with a smile.

"Oh, I just wanted to see how things were going," replied Mr. Snoops as he secretly hid a recording device under the examination table. He quickly left.

Doctor Doug talked to his animal patients all day as usual. When Mr. Snoops secretly took the recorder back and listened to it, he jumped for joy. "I finally got him!" he exclaimed.

The next day, the sun was shining, and the birds were singing their songs. This time when he arrived to work, Doctor Doug saw men in white coats taking Mr. Snoops away.

"What's going on?" Doctor Doug asked one of the men.

"This guy went to the police with a tape of animal noises claiming he knows someone who talks to animals. We think we need to send him away to be evaluated. Sometimes, these old people come up with crazy ideas. Hopefully, he'll be back before you know it," he replied.

IN WHICH WAYS ARE YOU SMART?

Answer the following questions, and then tally your "Yes" answers at the end.

1.	I like to help people all the time.	Yes	No
2.	I am good at taking care of flowers and plants.	Yes	No
3.	I work well in a group.	Yes	No
4.	I enjoy writing stories.	Yes	No
5.	Playing sports comes easily to me.	Yes	No
6.	In my bedroom, I often listen to music.	Yes	No
7.	Maps and graphs are easy for me to read.	Yes	No
8.	Many times, I just like to be alone.	Yes	No
9.	It's easy for me to see the patterns in things.	Yes	No
10.	I love to read books.	Yes	No
11.	I enjoy camping and the outdoors.	Yes	No
12.	I like to have time to myself to think.	Yes	No
13.	I love to dance.	Yes	No
14.	I play a musical instrument quite well.	Yes	No
15.	I like to draw.	Yes	No
16.	Beautiful photos and pictures make me happy.	Yes	No

Tally your "Yes" answers.

Nature # 2, 11	Number # 7, 9	Music # 6, 14	Body # 5, 13	Word # 4, 10	Picture # 15, 16	Self # 8, 12	People # 1, 3

For every box with two tally marks, this is a way you are smart. If you have more than three ways you are smart, try to think of the three that most appeal to you and describe you the best.

DOODLE-PREDICT SHEET

Selection: _____

Title: _____ Name: _____ Date: _____

Doodle: Draw a picture representing what you just read.	Predict: Write a complete sentence prediction of what will happen next in the story. Use specific details and character names.	Doodle: Draw a picture representing what you just read.
Predict: Write a complete sentence prediction of what will happen next in the story. Use specific details and character names.	Doodle: Draw a picture representing what you just read.	Did your predictions come true? Circle one: Yes No Explain in a complete sentence why your predictions came true or not. _____ _____ _____ _____ What is the *genre* of this selection? _____

9 A Final Note

The authors sincerely hope that many readers will finish this book filled with inspiration and determination to radically change their classrooms and that the start of the next teaching year will be heralded by educators moving their furniture, installing sound docks, creating math grids on the floor, and teaching memory pegs. If you are one of those teachers, welcome to the world of Green Light education! You may be the only teacher in your school trying these strategies—but you are not alone. There is a growing faculty of like-minded educators all over the world using Green Light strategies to stunning effect. You can find them by e-mailing info@greenlighteducation.net and asking to be put in touch with a Green Light mentor.

However, we also understand that other readers may not have the energy, resources, support, or time to implement the High-Five approach all at once. If your circumstances and challenges make radical change impossible, why not implement just *one* of the following ideas, even in a very limited way:

- **Math Grid:** If you're still going to use worksheets, at least introduce each concept on the grid first. Watch how the students who used to dislike math begin to engage with this approach.
- **Spelling Hopscotch:** If you can't use this as the primary teaching method, at least let students *practice* their spelling words by hopping them out. Notice how some previously hopeless spellers suddenly see the light.
- **Music:** If you can't have a sound track to the entire school day, at least start your day with upbeat music. You'll be amazed at the difference it makes.
- **Memory Pegs:** If you can't introduce this at the beginning of the school year, at least teach the pegs as a novelty "end of semester" activity. Next semester, you might then show your students how to memorize just one area of core content. See if your students do better than expected on the test.
- **Learning Locations:** If you can't move your furniture, or students *have* to work seated, at least allow movement between activities by asking learners to rotate to a different row or table. You'll probably find concentration levels improve almost immediately.

At its core, Green Light teaching is about doing something—anything—that seeks to improve student engagement, understanding, recall, and test results. Try just one idea, and evaluate it. If it works, do it again, and do it more! Perhaps try another strategy too. The results may not be as dramatic as they were in Cindy's classroom—but you *will* see them.

Whether you are planning to jump in at the deep end or just put an exploratory toe in the water, take heart from the fact that the rewards of Green Light teaching are powerful and profound. If you can make learning a fun and rewarding experience, you will break the dam that's holding your students back from succeeding in today's education system, and they will achieve beyond both your and their expectations.

Endnotes

1. For more ideas on alternative memory strategies to use, see Chapter 2 of *Green Light Classrooms* (Allen, 2008), which illustrates a plethora of entertaining and effective memorization techniques.

2. For more specific ideas on how to give effective directions, see Dr. Allen's (2010) book, *High-Impact Teaching in the XYZ Era of Education.*

3. This lesson is based on an original idea by Rob Jensen (2008b) in his book, *Catalyst Teaching,* and is presented here with his permission.

4. This idea is courtesy Estelle Bollen, of Wesley College, Perth, Australia.

References

Allen, R. H. (2008). *Green Light classrooms: Teaching techniques that accelerate learning.* Thousand Oaks, CA: Corwin.

Allen, R. H. (2010). *High-impact teaching Strategies in the 'XYZ' era of education.* Boston: Allyn & Bacon.

Allington, R. L. (2006). *What really matters for struggling readers: Designing research-based programs* (2nd ed.). Boston: Pearson Education.

Bartholomew, B. (2008). Sustaining the fire. *Educational Leadership, 65*(6), 55–60.

BrainyQuote. (2010). Dwight D. Eisenhower quotes. *BrainyQuote.* Retrieved April 11, 2010, from http://www.brainyquote.com/quotes/quotes/d/dwightdei 149111.html

BrainyQuote. (2010). Vince Lombardi quotes. *BrainyQuote.* Retrieved April 11, 2010, from http://www.brainyquote.com/quotes/authors/v/vince_lombardi.html.

Caine, R. N., & Caine, G. (1994). *Making connections: Teaching the human brain.* Menlo Park, CA: Addison-Wesley.

Coleman, E., Rivkin, I., & Brown, A. (1997). The effect of instructional explanations on learning from scientific texts. *Journal of the Learning Sciences, 6,* 347–365.

Cookson, P. W., Jr. (2009). What would Socrates say? *Educational Leadership, 67*(1), 8–14.

Crowe, C. (2008). Solving behavior problems together. *Educational Leadership, 66*(3), 44–47.

Drevets, W. C., & Raichle, M. E. (1998). Reciprocal suppression of regional cerebral blood flow during emotional versus higher cognitive processes: Implications for interactions between emotion and cognition. *Cognition & Emotion, 12,* 353–385.

Egan, K., & Judson, G. (2008). Of whales and wonder. *Educational Leadership, 65*(6), 20–25.

Fisher, D., & Frey, N. (2008). Releasing responsibility. *Educational Leadership, 66*(3), 32–37.

Freeley, M. E., & Hanzelka, R. (2009). Getting away from seat time. *Educational Leadership, 67*(3), 63–67.

Glasser, W. (1999). *Choice theory: A new psychology of personal freedom.* New York: HarperCollins.

Gray, J., Braver, T., & Raichle, M. (2002). Integration of emotion and cognition in the lateral prefrontal cortex. *Proceedings of the National Academy of Sciences of the United States of America, 99,* 4115–4120.

Hersh, R. H. (2009). A well-rounded education for a flat world. *Educational Leadership, 67*(1), 50–53.

Hollas, B. (2005). *Differentiating instruction in a whole-group setting: Taking the first easy steps into differentiation.* Peterborough, NH: Crystal Springs Books.

Jensen, E. (2006). *Enriching the brain: How to maximize every learner's potential.* San Francisco: Jossey-Bass.

Jensen, E. (2008a). *Brain-based learning: The new paradigm of teaching* (2nd ed.). Thousand Oaks, CA: Corwin.

Jensen, R. (2008b). *Catalyst teaching.* Melbourne, Australia: Harker Brownlow Education.

Jensen, E. (2009). *Fierce teaching: Purpose, passion and what matters most.* Thousand Oaks, CA: Corwin.

Jiaxu, C., & Weiyi, Y. (2000). Influence of acute and chronic treadmill exercise on rat brain POMC gene expression. *Medicine & Science in Sports & Exercise, 32*(5), 954–957.

Jing, J., Yuan, C., & Liu, J. (1999, May). Study of human figure drawings in learning disabilities. *Chinese Mental Health Journal, 13*(3), 133–134.

Kagan, S., & Kagan, M., (1998). *Multiple intelligences: The complete MI book.* San Clemente, CA: Kagan Cooperative Learning.

Klein, R. (2008). Engaging students around the globe. *Educational Leadership, 65*(6), 8–13.

Knecht, S., Breitenstein, C., Bushuven, S., Wailke, S., Kamping, S., Floel, A., et al. (2004). Levodopa: Faster and better word learning in normal humans. *Annals of Neurology, 56*(1), 20–26.

Krashen, S. (1982). *Principles and practice in second language acquisition.* New York: Oxford University Press.

Mandela, N. (1995). *Long walk to freedom.* Randburg, South Africa: Macdonald Purnell.

Mansilla, V. B., & Gardner, H. (2008). Disciplining the mind. *Educational Leadership, 65*(5), 14–19.

Marzano, R. J. (2007). *The art and science of teaching: A comprehensive framework for effective instruction.* Alexandria, Virginia: Association for Supervision and Curriculum Development.

Marzano, R. J., Pickering, D. J., & Pollock, J. E. (2001). *Classroom instruction that works: Research-based strategies for increasing student achievement.* Alexandria, VA: Association for Supervision and Curriculum Development.

Mitra, D. (2008). Amplifying student voice. *Educational Leadership, 66*(3), 20–25.

Nikola-Lisa, W. (2006). *How we are smart.* New York: Lee & Low Books.

O'Rourke, M., & Fletcher, K. (2004). *KidSmart early learning program Asia Pacific evaluation final report.* Strawberry Hills, New South Wales, Australia: The Australian National Schools Network.

Palinscar, A. S., & Brown, A. L. (1984). Reciprocal teaching in comprehension-fostering and comprehension-monitoring activities. *Cognition and Instruction, 1*(2), 117–175.

Peretz, I., & Zatorre, R. J. (2005). Brain organization for music processing. *Annual Review of Psychology, 56,* 89–114.

Polacco, P. (1998). *Thank you, Mr. Falker.* New York: Penguin Putnam.

Pressley, M., Dolezal, S., Raphael, L., Mohan, L. Roehrig, A., & Bogner, K. (2003). *Motivating primary grade students.* New York: Guilford.

Rossi, E. (2002). *Psychobiology of gene expression.* New York: W.W. Norton.

Sousa, D. (2001). *How the brain learns* (2nd ed.). Thousand Oaks, CA: Corwin.

Squire, L. R. (1992). Memory and the hippocampus: A synthesis from findings with rats, monkeys, and humans. *Psychological Review, 99*, 195–231.

Swartz, R. (2008). Energizing learning. *Educational Leadership, 65*(5), 26–31.

Tate, M. L. (2003). *Worksheets don't grow dendrites: 20 instructional strategies that engage the brain.* Thousand Oaks, CA: Corwin.

ThinkExist.Com. (1999–2010). Nelson Mandela quotes. *ThinkExist.Com.* Retrieved April 18, 2010, from http://thinkexist.com/quotation/as_a_leader-i_have_always_endeavored_to_listen_to/148828.html

Tomlinson, C. A. (1999). *The differentiated classroom: Responding to the needs of all learners.* Alexandria, VA: Association for Supervision and Curriculum Development.

Tomlinson, C. A. (2008). The goals of differentiation. *Educational Leadership, 66*(3), 26–30.

Tomlinson, C. A., & McTighe, J. (2006). *Integrating differentiated instruction + understanding by design: Connecting content and kids.* Alexandria, VA: Association for Supervision and Curriculum Development.

Van Praag, H., Christie, B. R., Sejnowski, T. J., & Gage, F. H. (1999). Running enhances neurogenesis, learning, and long-term potentiation in mice. *Proceedings of the National Academy of Sciences of the United States of America, 96*, 13427–13431.

Wessler, S. (2004). It's hard to learn when you're scared. *Educational Leadership, 61*(1), 40–43.

Winger, T. (2009). Grading what matters. *Educational Leadership, 67*(3), 73–75.

Wolfe, P. (2001). *Brain matters: Translating research into classroom practice.* Alexandria, VA: Association for Supervision and Curriculum Development.

Wolk, S. (2008). Joy in school. *Educational Leadership, 66*(1), 8–14.

Youth Sports Club. (2010). Vince Lombardi Page. Retrieved August 1, 2010, from www.footballcoachone.com/lombardi.html

Zmuda, A. (2008). Springing into active learning. *Educational Leadership, 66*(3), 38–42.

Index

CORWIN

A SAGE Company

The Corwin logo—a raven striding across an open book—represents the union of courage and learning. Corwin is committed to improving education for all learners by publishing books and other professional development resources for those serving the field of PreK–12 education. By providing practical, hands-on materials, Corwin continues to carry out the promise of its motto: **"Helping Educators Do Their Work Better."**